In My Own Time

CARRIE FINN

To Mia, Ava and Jack,

I dedicate this book to you three. You have taught me everything I need to know about life and I was meant to be the one teaching you.

My greatest privilege in life has been your mam. I love you more than you could imagine. I would do anything to protect you all. Thank you for giving me so much meaning and happiness in my life and showing me love and for opening your worlds to me. It has been the greatest role of my life being your mam. Love you to the moon and back.

To Daniel,

I dedicate this book to you, my love. Nothing about our journey has been simple. We made it work. Against all odds. If only 14 yr old us could see us now. We do everything in our own way and our own time. Its my favourite thing about us. Having you by myside, first as my best friend and then as the love of my life has made me the happiest woman every single day. You have always showed up for me in every way possible. You taught me what love is. You are the most amazing father that I could wish for all three of our babies. I hope you know how loved and adored you are. There are not enough words to say how very special you are to us and how much we love you. You deserve the world.

Table of Contents

CHAPTER 1

Early Childhood

MY mam told me I was clingy from the minute I arrived. I never left her alone. Her and my dad were my safe place and when I was with them, I did not have to try to be anyone but me.

My first memory is standing in our front garden aged three in our house in Loughlinstown Park, playing with my doll and buggy playing 'mammies.' Playing mammies was my favourite game for years. I would happily play away on my own for hours at a time in my made-up world. I was standing behind the gate in our garden that stopped us from running on to the estate. I was looking out at my older brother and sister playing away with their friends. I obviously did not know it at the time, but it would be the running theme in my life. Always looking into the world around me not realising how to fit into it. It was like I could not just open the gate and join in. I have felt different from other people my whole life. I never seemed to think like the other kids or read situations like they did, no matter how hard I tried. I have so many happy memories from my childhood despite feeling that way. I was the youngest of three.

My mam and dad had Karl first followed by my sister Toni. I came along a few years later. To this day Karl and Toni tell me that when they found out I was on the way, They were devastated to learn they would no longer have a bedroom each. I ruined the setup. Priorities and all that. As much as they pretended that I ruined their lives I never remember a time that they both were not always there for me. Karl had to drag Toni and I along wherever he went to play when my mam and dad were working. In the eighties we went out all day and came home when the streetlights came on. The innocent days before phones and Wi-Fi.

We would spend hours a day playing with everyone on our street. Only going home for dinner and then back out until bedtime. I have such fond memories of Loughlinstown Park. My mam worked part-time but always showed up to collect me from school, and always with a treat. Seeing her at the end of every school day used to instantly calm me as a child. The fire was always blazing when we got home and our favourite programme on the TV. Mam was always so present when she was with us. She always made me feel so loved and safe when she was around. I don't remember her ever not being there for all of us when we needed her. something I took for granted as a child, but now as a mother myself, I have huge gratitude and respect for her. She worked so hard and yet her care of us never waivered. I never remember her having a sick day or taking a day off. She always showed up. No matter what it was. Something I have carried through in my own Motherhood Journey. Always be present and always show up. Especially on the harder days. It sounds easy but it's so much more complex than people realise.

My dad was so hardworking but always found the time to do things with us. Some of my earliest and happy memories are my dad taking me on many walks and trying to give me all the life advice I needed, no matter how young I was. Those walks were another safe space for me. I felt so comfortable and so loved. He gave me his time even though he was always so busy. Yet he made that space for me. It meant so much to me that he did that. I felt like my dad knew deep down I always felt so different and full of anxiety and those times together eased that part of me. We would compare stories of those feelings and we really understood each other. I used to love our walks. He did all the talking and I tried to take in as much as possible.

Looking back on it now I did not know that I was constantly anxious and in flight or fight mode. I realise now there has not been a day that passes that I do not suffer with anxiety. It is such a debilitating disorder to live with. Dad was always the one I went to when I had an issue. I suffered from bullying for as long as I can remember, and it was always my dad I ran to, to fix it. He would, and then he'd tell me that my mouth gets me into trouble. I could not read social situations at all. I said the wrong things, always seeing situations in black and white in my head. I always felt like what I was saying or doing in those situations was the right thing, but then the other person would look at me like I was weird and saying something wrong. The world of social interactions and situations genuinely confused me and still do to this day. I was on another planet with my own language and they didn't understand me. No matter how much I tried to read their facial expressions or body language. I decided to either copy people's social queues and do all these extra helpful things that no one asked me to do. When I did that I felt like I really fitted in and people liked me for me. It gave me a sense of pride and happiness. Being kind to others genuinely made me happy but also made me feel accepted.

I went on to be a chronic people pleaser because of this very action. I realised that this was how I could cope with not fitting in. I copied how my cousins or sister acted,and just hoped I slotted into whatever situation we were in. This is something I only learnt I was doing when I saw the exact same behaviours in my own children. 20 years too late, but in the generation I grew up in no one spoke about anxiety, or feeling like they weren't the same as everyone else.

My mam adored living in Loughlinstown. She had great friends there, as did my dad. We had great times there. The neighbours, the street parties, the sense of community. Both my parents were originally from Sally noggin, and all dad ever wanted was to move back there. In his eyes Sally noggin was where his heart was. He wanted to be closer to his family too and just wanted to be back home. As much as he loved Loughlinstown and our life there he was determined to move back. Once Coach made up his mind about something it was a deal done. We were moving whether we wanted to or not. I remember him coming into my room when I had just turned 14, and telling me we were moving in two week's time to my Granny Gerties in Sallynoggin. I was shocked, but so excited too. At this time I was being chronically bullied. I had gone through sixth class and was continuously bullied to the point I took panic attacks walking to my mams car when she would collect me outside school. I will never forget how scared and alone I felt because of those two girls that did that to me. They would walk behind me, whispering about how they were going to beat me up after school, they would push and shove me in the hall or in the classroom. Always trying to intimidate me. I can still see their faces smiling and laughing as they saw me shaking. I was afraid to even go outside to play. It was months of that behaviour. They even followed me on the walk home to my Granny's and kept acting like they were going to attack me from behind. My whole body was shaking with fear. I actually ran ahead to a woman in front of me who was walking her dog and told her what was going on. She walked me the whole way to my granny's house. I'll never forget her kindness. It stopped after that as my mam contacted the school and their parents but it had a huge effect on my self-esteem which was already non-existent from being bullied in Loughlinstown.

For me, the move felt like a fresh start. An escape. I was super excited. We were already so close with my Granny, my mam's mother, spending every Saturday there with all my aunties and cousins. When we moved, I had to share a bedroom with my Granny for nine months as the house was old and needed to be extended to fit us all in. I loved it! She would tell me all the stories about her childhood, and we became even closer.

Granny Gertie worked till she was 80 in Graham O Sullivans Cafe in Dun Laoghaire. She would cycle down and up to work, and she had seven daughters. She had lost my Grandad many years before so was living alone when we moved in. She was a living legend and when I think now how she was so laid back about living with us all and sharing a room with a 14-year-old moody teenage girl. She really helped me settle into Sallynoggin. My best friend Michelle lived close to Sallynoggin too, and our move meant that we could see each other much more. We had been friends since fifth class, and 28 years later she is still one of my closest people in my life. I feel like my real friendships started in Sallynoggin.

CHAPTER 2

New Beginnings

We had been living in Granny Gerties for about two weeks when there was a knock on the door. I opened it and there was a boy standing there on his BMX bike and two boys and a girl standing at the gate smiling. He asked if I wanted to come out and play. I almost said no but my gut instinct was screaming to say yes. So, I did. That was the best choice I have ever made as it was the start of me falling in love. Although I didn't realise it back then. I dread to think how things would have turned out if I had let my anxiety win and said no.

Daniel Finn was the boy's name, and I knew at once that he was special. He had the kindest eyes I have ever seen. It felt like my heart was connected to his. I had never felt a connection like it before. I had no idea how much that knock on the door was going to change my life. It was the beginning of the best memories for me with an excellent group of friends. It was my first real group of genuine friends. I fitted in with them. I have such good memories of that time. Sallynoggin holds such great memories for me, of my teen years. We spent the entire summer together in a big group. Getting up to all sorts that we shouldn't have been. Including hopping over the wall into the local private golf course trying not to get caught which ended in disaster as I had a glowing yellow shirt on and fell over the wall landing on the ground. The boys were no help as they were too busy laughing at us. Myself and Amanda, one of the girls who I had become super close to, decided to hide behind trees that had no branches when we heard the golfers coming! We obviously weren't using our brains back then.

We fell around the course laughing, relieved we had not been caught. We spent many summer nights up in the football field all huddled together drinking cheap bottles of cider thinking we were so cool. Two bottles between about ten of us that one of the lads had been brave enough to ask the older lads to get for us in the off licence. I still shudder when I drink cider. It was rotten but great fun with all the gang!. I've only ever seen my dad lose his temper at me once to the point I was scared of him and that was that summer. One of the lads in the group had a free house. Very rare back then. We all said we would stay there and tell our parents we were sleeping in each other's houses. Foolproof plan. Or so we thought. Myself and

Michelle had said we were sleeping in our friends Stephanie's house and vice versa to her parents. That night I decided to drink vodka for the first time. I stupidly drank it like it was water and in no time at all the whole house was spinning around me. I ended up throwing up all night. Michelle had to put me in the shower and wash all the stuff out of my hair and Gary, the guy whose house was free, was panicking that his mam would find the towels. I finally fell asleep at six am and woke up four hours later with a hangover from hell. I haven't touched vodka since. We went down to Stephanie's house to see her only to be met by her mam looking really annoyed. She had rang my mam on our house phone to check if Stephanie was indeed sleeping over only for my mam to say 'No, Carrie is sleeping at your house?'. We had been caught out. To make it worse they had phoned at 7pm the previous night and we still had not arrived home. We didn't have mobile phones at that stage so they had no idea where we all were. We nearly dropped at the front door when she told us.

We were terrified to face my mam and dad. We decided the smart thing to do would be to walk to the local shop and stock up on sweets and chocolate because once we got home I would be grounded for life if my dad had his way. We crept up to my front door and took a deep breath and as I put my hand on the handle to open it the door flew open. My mam was standing there white as a ghost and staring right through us. She only said these words to us. 'Your Dad is inside waiting for you' and walked into the kitchen, closing the door. We were shaking. He absolutely lost it with both of us. He used to treat Michelle like one of his own and he gave out to her like that too. I was not allowed out for a month. He never budged on it. At the time I felt like he totally overreacted. Now as a parent how that has come back to bite me on the ass. If I can't see my own kids on their snapchat maps I panic instantly. Karma. I suddenly got his fear. Those times together with my friends are still some of my favourite memories even with all the carnage we caused. They were my first group of friends that I truly felt myself with. No bullying was heaven for that time in my life. I lived for school to be done each day so I could go out to my friends. That is all you want when you are a teenager, your friends become your whole world. I was still close to my mam and dad, but my relationship with them changed slightly as I grew up. Back then you *absolutely did not* tell your parents about what you got up to hence my drinking story.

School was always a real struggle for me and I don't know how I made it through. The only class I loved was English. I struggled majorly with Irish and maths. I dreaded going in most days, but especially if Michelle was not in. We stuck together like glue, and I couldn't bear facing lunchtime without her. I didn't have a clique in school. She was my only friend bar one other girl Claire who we would pal around with sometimes. I always felt lonely and sad there. I would often go to the toilet and sit there alone just so I wouldn't have to eat lunch alone at my table while everyone else always seemed to have someone. I was always shaking with anxiety the entire day. I hated the constant feeling of being overwhelmed and sad there. Again, back then I just assumed everyone felt like that in school and it was just one of those things you had to get on with. It is only now I realise I had a chronic anxiety disorder which I was finally diagnosed with in 2008. We did not even know the word anxiety when we were growing up. I didn't learn about anxiety until I had my own kids years later. I barely went into school in 5th year. I faked notes and went mitching constantly. Anything to escape that loneliness. I wanted to quit so badly but that was not even a thought I would put to my parents. It would have been a hard no. I was working part time in Graham O Sullivans. My nanny had got me the job and I loved it even though I would be so anxious cleaning the tables and serving the food. It really helped me become independent. Michelle worked around the corner in O'Briens so we would time our lunch breaks together. My goal was to get through school and get a full-time job. I had no idea what I wanted to do college wise or work wise. All I cared about was my social life with my friends. I didn't feel anxious with them. Everywhere else I did. It was a miracle I passed my leaving cert. I got good grades thanks to Daniel helping me study at my front door step.

The innocence we had. We so desperately wanted to grow up, yet had no idea of the pure lightness of not having any adult responsibilities. Those years, from 13 to 18, is the last time I remember feeling that lightness. Undamaged, as yet, from the curveballs life throws you. Now I feel as though I have lived through two different lives. One before tragedy, and one after.

When I hit 18, my entire world came crashing down. Suddenly my life was split into two different worlds and things were never the same. My innocent life was gone forever.

CHAPTER 3

Coach

We always called Dad by his nickname. His real name is Anthony but everyone ever knew him as Coach. It was his nickname as a kid as he adored cowboy and indian films when he was younger and one of the characters he loved was called Coach. His hobby was to rewatch all those movies on his day off. Mam and Dad had fallen madly in love as teenagers, They both were from the same area and it was love at first sight. If there was a definition of true love it was them. Even as a young child I knew what they had together was special. I always wanted to be like them when I grew up. They built a great life together and had a great social life . They adored their weekends out with their friends and we always had the best house parties for any occasion going. We were now living in Sallynoggin for four years and my dad was thrilled.

He loved living so closely to his brothers and his friends. Dad had a huge family and was one of ten children. He had eight brothers and one sister. He lost his own parents when he was very young in sudden circumstances. He was super close to all of his siblings and loved seeing them as much as possible . They were suddenly able to go to places and not worry about us since we were so much older now. I was eighteen, Toni 21 and Karl nearly 23 .My mam and dad were laid back about us going out if we got up for college and work. There was no such thing as laying around in bed late or having an 'off day'. We just didn't do that in our generation. Coaches biggest pet peeve was you sitting around doing nothing. Especially in Pjs after morning time. We did not dare go downstairs in our PJs hungover. It was dads one rule, and he was super strict about it. Which is ironic because anyone that knows me knows that I live in my pajamas. I hate having to get dressed to go out, my little rebellious streak against Coach's no pjs downstairs rule. I'm at my most relaxed in my pjs in my house. As soon as I get home for the day and I don't have to go back out I will straight away pop them on. It's a running joke in my house that I am to be buried in my Posh Pjs or I will come back and haunt my family. Sorry Coach I always did know how to wind you up!.

Dad was a huge fan of New York, he adored it. The first time my dad took us out of Ireland was on a trip to New York to visit his best friend Thomas, who had moved there years before. Thomas was like another brother to dad, and my dad adored him, his wife Sheila and their two kids. His face would light up talking about them. NewYork was one of my favourite holidays with him. He was so comfortable over there it was like his second home. Him and Mam went over so many times throughout the years. His friendships meant alot to him. Thomas and our neighbour Pat were his best friends. He adored living across the road from Pat and Libby in Loughlinstown and he really missed them when we moved down to Sallynoggin. They made a huge effort to see each other every week as mam and Libby were the best of friends too. We spent all of our childhood with them and their kids and we have some of the best memories with them. The house parties, the street parties were all great times. We all went on holidays together. When I think of Dads happiest times it was always with his friends or family. It was what mattered most to him. Something he has passed on to me. Our two families were super close and still are to this day. Coach loved a good party. Any excuse to get out and see everyone and embarrass us with his dad dancing.

My cousin turned 18 in April of 2003. She had a big party and my dad made me get up and dance to 'Sweet Caroline.'That was our song because I was going to be called Caroline, but Carrie was picked instead. I can still see us dancing, and remember thinking then how much I loved him. I left the party to go to the nightclub with friends and Coach was slagging us saying he wanted to come down with us to act cool. I remember sitting in the taxi with my friend at the time and saying to her how much I loved him and how he always had the craic with us. He loved to slag people over anything, this time it was my friend's highlights she had just gone done. He kept slagging her saying who had put stripes into her head. Typical Dad joke behaviour. Laughing more at himself then us actually laughing at him. He could be savage with the jokes. I had no idea that was the last time I would ever dance with my dad at a party. Someone snapped a photo of us as we finished dancing and thank God they did as it was the last photograph I have of us together. It is in my wallet ever since, and is one of my most prized possessions.

CHAPTER 4

The worst day of my life

May 19th, 2003, started out like any other day. I was thrilled I had a sleep in as I had been badly hung over the day before. I had turned 18 five weeks prior and really thought I was a grown-up. I was loving college life and the social outings that came with it. I was constantly out dancing and partying. Which Coach was not happy about. I also thought he was hung over as he had been out the weekend too, but he did not feel too well. He was working constantly, as he had only told us weeks previously that he was taking us to Australia for my cousin's wedding. We were all so excited. We had never been somewhere so far away. To go with our other family members was a huge bonus. The plan was to go for three weeks so the pressure was really on Coach and Mam to save for it. He was constantly taking extra shifts at the factory he worked at. On his days off he would be doing painting jobs or anything he could do to save money. He was always such a diligent worker. Something he and my mam both instilled in us. I had my first job when I was 14.. The three of us worked from the time we were young. It was not an option either. My first job was collecting glasses in a pub, then I worked in a hairdressers on a saturday which I loved. Then on to Graham o'sullivans with my granny and then on to Super Valu on the tills.

The house was quiet that day. Toni was away on holidays in Spain with her boyfriend at the time, and two other friends. Mam was at work, and my Nanny was home with me. Dad was gone to paint this lady's house in Bray. I can't remember where Karl was. I can only tell my version of that day and how it went from my perspective. I still remember every single detail of it. I woke up to my Aunty Dolores and Uncle Bisto coming in the front door. Dolores was my moms sister who married Dads brother Bisto. We were all super close. I could hear them go into my Granny in the kitchen and I could hear her shouting 'Oh no', but I had never heard her voice like that.

Instantly I got a weird feeling. My heart sped up. I could hear it thumping in my ears. It was so loud, my stomach started to do somersaults. I just knew something bad had happened. My aunty Dolores came into my room and sat down near me and said that my dad was in the hospital and he was not feeling well. I can still see her face. She looked so sad and so scared, but was trying to put on a brave face for me. I thought back to the night before. My dad had said he thought he was getting the flu and was getting an early night. I remember thinking he was off, but I assumed it was a hangover as he had been out the weekend with my mam. I got up and got dressed quickly, all the while thinking he would be fine. My dad was the strongest person I knew. Surely, he would be fine. I got in the car and I kept ringing his phone but no answer. I asked my uncle to stop at the shop so I could get my dad phone credit. I then sent him a text message to say I was on my way and that he was working too hard and had to stop. I told him I loved him and ended the message with a kiss.

As we drove into the entrance of St. Columcille's hospital in Loughlinstown, the first person I saw was my mam. She was sitting on the ground with her head in her hands. She was crying hysterically . I had never seen her like that. She looked broken, tortured like. I looked past her and saw my brother standing in a small window in the hospital. My cousins and aunties were with him. I remember wondering why everyone was there. My dad just had the flu. I clocked eyes with my brother, and at the same time I could hear mam saying the words 'He is gone, your dads gone. I am sorry.' My first thought was, where? He would not leave us, I knew, but as I looked at my brother I realised what she meant. My dad had died. It was like the world was spinning and crashing around me trying to process what was actually happening. Everything was in slow motion. I heard someone let out a wolf-like scream and then realised it was me doing it. It was a strange howling scream filled with sadness and shock and rage. I had never felt an emotion like that before. It was the most horrific feeling I have ever had. Karl engulfed me in this big hug when I entered the room where he was sitting with other family members. We seemed to sit in that hug for a long time but I'm sure it was only minutes.It was so quiet you could hear a pin drop. I kept waiting for someone to say they had made a mistake, but no one did. We sat there for a while getting increasingly numb and then we were called in to see my dad. My uncle Davy was there with me Dads brother, and Karl and I remember him just looking so broken. Seeing everyone so upset was so surreal. I wish in a way I could say I do not remember seeing my dad's body for the first time, but I do. It is an image that will haunt me forever. I had never seen a dead body before. He was on a silver table and the floor was messy with bits of tissues covered in blood and things they had obviously used. I will never forget putting my hand on his head and feeling how cold he was. It made me jump back. It was like I only realised then he was really gone. He had this half smile on his face as if he had just seen someone he loved. He looked peaceful. He had hard blood on his ear. In my head I was screaming at him to wake up. I even shook his arm a little but nothing. Just that stone cold feeling of his skin. I was devastated.

My Dad went to work that morning and had a cardiac arrest. The lovely woman who he was painting asked him if he wanted a cup of tea and when she came back into the living room, he was gone. He was 46..

After the hospital I felt like everything was in slow motion. We went home at some stage, and the house was full of family and friends. I could not breathe with the complete sense of shock and overwhelm. I remember ringing one of my friends at the time, Ashling, and her mam Pat answered. Pat told me years later she thought I had been attacked. I was so hysterical she could not make out what I was saying. I was in complete shock.

I walked over to meet one of my other friends after work. That is how in shock I was. I did not know what to do or what to say. Neither did anyone else. They came back to my house with me, and I was afraid to go to bed that night. I did not want to sleep alone so one of my college friends stayed with me. Toni was trying to get a flight home. I could not stop thinking of her. She was always super close with my dad and her being so far away seemed to make it even more cruel. When she pulled up outside the house the next day, we went out to meet her from the car as the house was packed full of people. I watched my mam hug her so tightly and Toni just looked broken. I had never seen her look so sad. She went straight upstairs away from everyone. It was all too much. No one knew how to act.

Our house was full of people for those three days after he died. I already knew he was so loved but the crowds that paid their respects to him showed us just how popular he was too. Everyone was as shocked as us to lose him so suddenly and so cruelly. We took my dad home so people could come and say their goodbyes, and there was an endless stream of visitors. Constant pots of tea and food being served. Everyone shared their stories of Coach, tears followed by laughter as someone told a funny story about him. Silence followed as it sunk in that there would never be new stories with him in it. Those first few days were filled with strange feelings of absolute heartbreak, confusion, sadness and trying to be strong for our family. No one tells you how to cope with such loss. Let alone losing a parent. It's unimaginable till it happens. I was blessed with great friends around me at that time. I would not have gotten through it without them. They were my rock. Suddenly the carefree life of being a college student had ended so abruptly. I felt like all my family lost a version of ourselves that day that we could never get back. You can never return to the same person you were. Your life splits into two different versions. Your old one and your new one. Especially when you lose someone so suddenly. It was so unexpected. No warning signs. It was just a normal day. Till it was not. Our life as a family of five was over that day. Our new life would only have four.

It felt like someone had ripped all the innocence out of the world for me. I found myself looking at every single situation in my life so differently. How could anything ever possibly be normal again? The life we had was over. We could never be who we were again. It was stolen from us in the most heart wrenching way possible. We didn't just lose Coach that day, we lost ourselves. I decided to speak at the funeral. I felt like I owed it to my dad. I wanted him to know how much I loved him. I tried to think about what to write down. I thought about the last words spoken between us. It seemed surreal that we had just been chatting about our weekends out and now two days later I was trying to write a eulogy about him. When I was little, my dad and I had a secret handshake. Every night before bed we would do the handshake. When I was sixteen, we stopped doing it. I thought I was too cool to do it any more. The night before my dad died, for some reason I will never know, when we said good night I went over to him and we did the handshake. The smile on his face. We said goodnight and I love you. Those were my last words to him. Ever. I cannot express how relieved I am to this day our last words were not out of anger or tiredness. They were true happy words.

I did not put that in my writing piece in the end. It was something I wanted to treasure. Instead of writing a speech, I wrote a letter to Coach. It felt more personal, and it felt right. I was so nervous about getting up and speaking in front of the whole church.

The day of Coach's funeral I remember driving from the house up to the church in the noggin, only five minutes away and the car park had over one hundred people there waiting as the church inside was already full. It really warmed my heart. Dad would have loved how popular he was. Out of everyone in the crowd the first person I spotted was Daniel. We had gone our separate ways the year I went to college. We had not really spoken. Ventured off on different paths, as people do. I really missed seeing him each day. Yet there he was. Standing at the church. It meant so much to me that he was there. The funeral went on for two hours. When I finally got up to speak, I was shaking. The anxiety was making me feel dizzy and nauseous. I decided to pretend the church was empty and it was just me reading a letter to my dad. I got through it and jumped back to reality when I heard over two hundred people clapping.

Coach was so adored by so many. That is what I took from that day. He was not just my dad. He was a husband, a brother, a friend, a work colleague, and a neighbour. Everyone was just as crushed as us. We went on to the crematorium then and the service was full of his favourite songs.

'The town I loved so well' by the Dubliners blasted out of the speakers as he went behind the curtain. I felt like half my heart went with him. It took me about 15 years to be able to listen to that song again without breaking down. If I heard sweet Caroline at a party, I usually ended up in the toilet crying. It is all those trivial things that hit you unexpectedly, even years later. You'll see their favourite bar in the shop and go to buy it only to remember he isn't here to eat it. Something good will happen and you pick up the phone to tell them all about it remembering he doesn't have a phone to call. You'll take a picture of a family occasion and search for them in the photo. The sadness knocks the wind out of you every single time.

I honestly do not know how any of us got through those few days. We were always a close family but losing Coach bonded us all together in the grief and devastation. We all dealt with it in our own ways. My way? Run and try avoiding it. To face it was to feel the unbearable emotions of grief, sadness, loss, and I would have to accept that he was gone. So, I escaped mentally from it all. I ran so far that I did not recognise myself for the seven months after he died. Until I had no choice but to face reality.

CHAPTER 5

The Darkness

Two weeks after Coach died, I returned to work. The house was so different now he was gone. It was just so quiet. I thought going back to work would be a distraction. I was working part-time in the local Supermarket then, and had just finished College. I was now qualified as a Medical Secretary, but I had absolutely no idea what I wanted to actually do with my life.

When I wasn't at work, I spent most of my time going out and drinking with my friends. They had so much patience with me back then. As soon as I was drunk the tears would start. They would all hug me, try to get me to talk to them, but I felt like I was in a different world than they were . I wasn't the same Carrie I had been just weeks before. No matter how much I tried to be. All the innocence of life before tragedy had been sucked out of me. It was like watching everyone living their lives stuck behind a sheet of glass. The world went on but not with us in it. We seemed frozen in time. Our world was full of grief. I would go to work, go out drinking, then fall into bed in the early hours. It continued like that for a long time. I was desperate to escape the sadness in the house. We all grieve in our own way, and this was mine. I didn't know how to go back to 'normal'. I didn't know how I was meant to carry on. The grief was so overwhelming that I just wanted to get away from it all the time. At home it was there waiting for me. Making me feel the pain and trauma. The more I went out the more I felt I was running away from it but as soon as I got drunk there it was. Loud and aggressive and taking hold of me. Insisting I feel it all. I couldn't seem to run far enough away for it not to follow me.

None of us had ever been through something so traumatising before. We did not know how to grieve, I guess. I remember hearing my mam crying in her room, when she thought I was out. She was absolutely broken. She had lost her soul mate. Her entire world. Nothing we could say would change that. She would come down and put a brave face on for us, but I knew how sad she was. I hated that I couldn't help her, I couldn't fix it.

Anger soon replaced the sadness, and I found myself angry at everything and everyone. Including my dad. I would scream at him in my head – How could he leave us? How could he rip our world apart like this? I obviously knew deep down it was not his fault, but try telling that to an immature 18 year-old that had never before been rocked by life. I had lost the person who fixed everything for me. How could life go on? It seemed inhumane for us to be able to carry on. It was impossible and I could not cope with the darkness and heaviness of it all.

No one tells you the stages of grief. Looking back, after dealing with my grief properly through counselling, I see them now and know it was all so normal to feel that way. But at that time I was a frightened kid just trying to run away from all it entailed. It frightened me so much.

The next seven months I was barely at home. I ended up dating one of the lads from work. The relationship was toxic from the start, and looking back I can see that it made everything worse. I stayed in his house a lot to escape my own. Not the best environment to be in. In my head, anything was better than facing the reality of Coach never coming back. I wanted an escape all the time.

My mam took us on that trip to Australia in August. A break we all desperately needed after the last few months. I do not know how she found the strength, but she did. We spent five weeks there. She gave us the most wonderful trip. It was another escape from reality in a way. We went with my family My Auntie Collette (my mum's sister) , Uncle Paul and my cousin Jamie. It was their son getting married in Australia.

Their family on Paul's side came too and we all got on so well. I adored Sue and Georgie and their baby George. He was such a welcome distraction from all the heartache. I bonded with him so much and he brought out a maternal side in me I didn't know I even had. Sue had lost her dad previously so we bonded over our mutual loss. She was my guardian angel on that trip. She really got me through the days. She has the purest soul and heart. She is the most amazing mother. I still adore her to this day. She was the light on some of my darkest days. She taught me alot about love and support on that trip. We spread some of dad's ashes on Bondi Beach. He had been so looking forward to this trip it felt right to place him there. We went to my cousin's wedding. We spent days in the pool. We ate out at lovely restaurants. We did different day trips. Like another world. They were like an alternative reality, those few short weeks. Sunshine and happiness. A world away from the heartache we had left at home. We were in our own little bubble surrounded by our own support system with our family. We really needed that level of support and understanding at such a horrible time. We felt cocooned by them all.

I went back to college in September, to do a journalism course. I always wanted to be a writer. This was my chance. Michelle, my childhood best friend, was also in that college. We spent most days not going in. I just could not focus when I was there. Instead we would go to McDonald's for breakfast, stroll around Dun Laoghaire and go home that evening, or I would get the bus straight up to the boyfriend's house. I suppose I felt like the toxic environment with him was better than going home to a house without my dad.. That is how my brain worked at that time. Escapism was my answer to everything. If I was not around at home I wouldn't feel the pain as hard. I could distract myself easily away from my family. I ran towards anything other than them. My brain could not process the trauma at all.

The college ended up calling my mam and told her I was never in. She was raging. Rightly so. I didn't miss many days after that phone call (and a big telling off by mam!). I started going in a lot more and found that I actually enjoyed the course. It was so nice to have structure and some routine. Writing for me has always been one of my favourite hobbies so choosing Journalism as a course was a no brainer for me. I had always written stories from the time I was little so it was refreshing to have that drive back. My tutor really tried to push my abilities and wanted me to succeed.

I did, however, quit my job. Purely for selfish reasons. I was so hungover all the time that I did not wake up to go in. I was in dangerous territory.

As December came in, I was starting to finally wake up to the fact that I really was not in a good space. Or a good relationship. It was as toxic as it could be. I found the thoughts of the first Christmas without dad unbearable. He had absolutely adored Christmas. He was like a big child that way. He loved his birthday just as much. He would mark off all the days on the calendar, hyper with the thoughts of his big day. Something that he has passed on to me. We celebrate birthdays big in my house, balloons, decorations and a big fuss no matter the age. We carry on his traditions that way. His excitement about them lives through us.

Christmas without him was creeping in, and I seemed to dive even further into the dark. The night before Christmas Eve I went out with friends. They all headed home early, and I remember sitting down, alone and drunk, on the path facing the Sallynoggin hill near our house. I cried and cried until I thought I had no tears left. It took everything I had to physically drag myself home that night. I can still see myself feeling so broken. I did not want to tell my family how I felt. I knew that they were feeling just as bad as I was. That was one of the lowest points in my life. Sitting alone like that. I felt worthless and really struggled with dark thoughts that night. I really felt like I was absolutely drowning and there was no life jacket nearby to save me and even if there had been I am not sure I wanted to be saved. I just wanted the pain to disappear fully. I was so ashamed of how I had been lashing out. I had become the most selfish person. Never home. Never fully present when I was home. I did not recognise myself when I looked in the mirror, but I couldn't seem to find my way forward. The Darkness engulfed me. I couldn't find a way out. I felt like I was screaming for help but no one could hear me.

That first Christmas was so wretched. It was a long hard dark day that we tried to get through. There really are no words for the firsts of every occasion. It just feels like your heart is being freshly ripped in two. They say time is a healer. I disagree. You never fully heal. You just learn a new way of living without that person over time. A new life. You must leave the old one behind. Life goes on around you and you either sit with your grief and try to understand it or you disappear into it and you may never come out the otherside. Grief is the price you pay for love.

The one positive of that month was that I split from my boyfriend. I had finally come to my senses. It was an unbelievably bad place to be in and I finally hit a wall with it all. It was a very unhealthy relationship. I was being used, lied to and treated really badly. My self esteem was non-existent and I felt trapped in it. I am proud that I had the courage to get away from it. It left me very damaged. I wanted to head into the new year focusing on myself. Getting myself better. Be there for my own family. Work through all the trauma of losing Dad. I got a part time job working in Tesco on the tills. It was in the local shopping centre so it was always busy, and a good distraction. It was the fresh start I needed… until I realised my period was late. Not the new beginning I had planned after all.

CHAPTER 6

Reality Check

I instantly felt the anxiety and fear running through me when I checked my calendar. My period was a week late. I was shaking buying the pregnancy test. I felt like the whole chemist was watching me. I went up to the toilet in the shopping centre where I worked, and read the instructions that came with the test. I kept saying to myself, *why am I even doing a test? There is no way I could be pregnant.* Those were the longest three minutes of my life. When it flashed up pregnant, I thought I was going to faint. My whole body was shaking. I couldn't take it in, and I couldn't believe it.I went and bought another two tests thinking the first one must be wrong. I got the bus home with Michelle and thankfully no one was in my house. I did both new tests, and of course the cross for positive and the word pregnant appeared again. There was no denying it now. Michelle was as shocked as me. We sat in stunned silence for ages and then she eventually had to get the last bus home. I made her take the boxes from the tests with her so she could put them in the bin at the bus stop where no one would find them. I hid the tests in my handbag. We were so naive. We really had no idea.

I couldn't sleep a wink that night. I kept going over and over in my head what I was going to do. On my way to work the next morning there was a poster on the bus for a helpline to call if you found yourself pregnant and did not know the next steps. I rang the number, and when someone answered I panicked and hung up. I was too afraid to speak about it. I was worried someone on the bus would hear me. I didn't know what to say either. I felt like if I said out loud to the person on the phone it would make it more real.

I went into work in a complete daze. I arranged a doctor's appointment for later that day in the hope that the tests were wrong. The doctor was lovely and supportive. She confirmed what the tests already had. I was going to have a baby. I was 18 and alone. I was terrified. Toni was away for the weekend, so I went and stayed at my friend Ashling's house. Ashling was as shocked as me but so supportive. I will never forget how kind and supportive her mam was when we told her. Pat was so good to me. That kindness stuck with me all my life, and now when any of my kids are in challenging situations I often resort back to her way and use it myself. She didn't judge, she didn't look at me with disgust. She just sat and listened. She held my hand and let me be afraid. She didn't shame me. She was there for me in the way I needed at that moment.

I thought Toni would never get home so I could confide in her. I burst out crying when I told her the next day. Saying it aloud somehow made it seem more real. She instantly hugged me and told me I would be okay. She was shocked but didn't let that stop her trying to make me feel better. I really needed that support, and I am so glad she was the first one I told in my family. She just held space for me with no judgment.

I was terrified to tell my mam. No one wants to disappoint their parents. She had only lost my dad eight months before. She was already going through so much. I will never forget the dread I felt waiting to tell her. Toni and I sat at the kitchen table while mam was cooking. She was chatting away to us about her day. I felt like the words were stuck in my throat, I could not get them out. I thought she had to be able to hear my heart beating out of my chest, it was that loud in my ears. My whole body was shaking with anxiety. I knew how disappointed she would be. I had not been around much the last eight months and here she was thinking I was finally getting myself back on track. I kept trying to speak but it was like my throat kept closing up. Toni was just staring at me from the other end of the table, willing me to speak but looking as scared as I felt. I took a deep breath in and finally spoke. I managed to say to her that I needed to tell her something and could she sit down. She sat down beside me and jokingly said 'you're not pregnant are you'. My heart seemed to fall out of my chest when she said that. I just stared at her and said, 'yes I am.' It was like she reacted in slow motion. She initially looked shocked, then angry, and then sad. Then I got upset looking at her reaction. It was like she was feeling all the emotions at once. She looked at Toni in disbelief and then back to me and said, 'What did you just say?' I was even more scared repeating it the second time. I said 'I;m pregnant and I am sorry'. I started to cry as all the fear took over me. She sat down and put her head in her hands and said 'what have you done?' She was devastated. She looked broken again. The shame washed over me. I have never felt so ashamed as I did in that moment. I had broken her heart. Again. It stuck with me for a long time afterwards. The guilt of it all. It really affected me and how I saw myself for many years later.

I can put myself in her shoes now being the mother of teenagers. She always apologises for her initial reaction all these years later, but I totally understand it. Her youngest daughter had just told her life changing news, eight months after her husband had suddenly died. She was absolutely overwhelmed with it all, and rightly so. She might have had a few weeks of a bad reaction, but she gave me a lifetime of support after. She has nothing to feel bad for. I can never repay her for all the love and support she gave me and Mia from the very beginning. She was my saviour once the dust settled. She showed up for me in all the ways that I needed. She taught me the true meaning of a mothers love. She brought me back to life in one of the hardest and darkest times of her life.

I remember while telling everyone about my pregnancy I had this overwhelming sense of shame and guilt. I genuinely believed I had brought such shame on my family, and that cut me deeply. I was the youngest and caused the most chaos. I told my brother next. I went in and sat on Karl's bed and told him. He did not look shocked or annoyed. If he was, he did not show it. Instead, he instantly told me he would support me and be there. I cried and cried after that. I really needed to hear that. Mam, Karl and Toni became my other half in that pregnancy. The biggest support system I could have had. They stepped in and were there.

Granny, I was petrified of telling. She was of the fierce old school generation. I sat down beside her in her little sitting room and I told her. She took my hand and whispered in my ear, 'Carrie you will not be the first and you certainly will not be the last. You will be fine.' I could not believe how well she took it. I was bringing a baby into her house. I was going to be bringing huge change to the entire house and she was so cool about it. I am sure in private she was worried sick about it all, but she never once let that on to me.

Telling my ex I was pregnant was a terrible experience. I left his house that day knowing full well I was going to be on my own with this baby. He was arrogant and aggressive in his responses to me. He tried to make me feel like I was not worth the dirt on his shoes. Him and his dad demanded a DNA test. I walked out of that house knowing in my soul I would never ever let another man treat me like that again. I never stepped foot in that house again after that meeting. Being pregnant changed something in me. It created the mother in me. It created a fire in me to do everything in my power for both of us. I had never had that feeling before. I think carrying this baby genuinely saved my life. It was the light in the darkness after dad died. I suddenly realised it was me and this baby now against the world. That is how it felt at the time. This baby was my purpose in life. It was knowing I was going to have to step up for a baby that pulled me out of that darkness. She deserved the best possible start in life. She deserved a healthy and healed mother. I was not going to bring her into my world filled with trauma and pain. It ended there with me. We both deserved a fresh start surrounded by love and happiness. No matter the circumstances.

I was determined to be the best mother possible. My age did not come into it for me as an obstacle. It was like I suddenly knew why I was here. I was meant to be this baby's mother. I took all the shame and guilt I felt and I turned it into love and determination.

I went to visit Sue at her house in Ballybrack because she had been such an influence on me in Australia. She was reassuring and encouraging, and spoke so positively to me. That is what I needed. I could only hope I would be half the mother she was. It was lovely to have that guidance along with the support from my own family. Those supportive conversations healed a lot in me.

I suffered with the most horrendous morning sickness the entire pregnancy. I was constantly admitted to hospital and hooked up to drips, as I was so dehydrated from vomiting. Nothing about the pregnancy was easy. I was still attending college and working part-time. It was hard being pregnant in college. A lot of stares, whispers. Not the nicest feeling. I used to constantly dive below my till in work to my bin with nausea. I could barely hold my head up some days. I would constantly have to hop off the bus to vomit or get air. I had no energy and dragged myself to work and college. It was grueling. I'd end the days barely able to hold my head up. I was so ill and tired.

I finished college in April. My dream of being a journalist was gone. I had to focus on this baby. I worked full-time right up until my maternity leave despite the illness. I saved every penny I could to buy everything I needed. My mam attended every hospital appointment and every scan. She was my biggest cheerleader, and it changed our relationship for the better. I suddenly could see things from her perspective, now that I was going to be a mother too. I found out I was having a girl and went looking in the baby names book. I instantly fell in love with the name Mia. It meant 'mine.' It was perfect.

I was still going out most weekends, but I did not drink. I just loved to dance, pregnant or not. I refused to miss a night out as I knew soon that I would need a babysitter just to have a shower. I went out my entire pregnancy until two weeks before my due date. I was just happy to be out with my friends feeling like I was not missing too much. We would end every night out sitting at Alex's, the local shop, where I would drink tea and eat golden crisp bars at three in the morning. Golden crisps were one of my cravings. I lived off ice cream, golden crisps and fig roll biscuits. I could not get enough of them, even with all the sickness. I was treasuring only minding myself in those moments. All too soon those days would be gone.

It was always at night when the busyness of the day was over that I would get scared about having a baby alone. I had no idea what was ahead of me. The unknown and the fear would set in. I knew I already loved this baby girl so much and I had not even met her yet. I cherished the feeling of lying in my bed and feeling her kick all night long. She obviously did not like to sleep at night either. I would try and picture what she would look like, who she would be. Would we be close? Would she hate me for how she had come into the world? Would my love be enough? Would I be enough?.

The house was ready for her, just about. I had saved enough money to buy a second hand buggy and car seat. My mam bought Mia her Moses basket, Toni and Karl bought me a steriliser and bottles and a lot of baby clothes. My Granny bought the cot. I would buy nappies and clothes each week when I got paid. I stocked up on formula, baby books, anything else I could think of. I was ready for her to arrive . My whole life was about to change. I had no idea just how much it really all would change. It was going to be a whole new beginning for me. It was my second chance at a happier life.

CHAPTER 7

Along came Mia

Mia Adrienne Burton came into the world 10 days past her due date on the 9th of October 2004 at 15.40pm weighing 6lbs 4 ounces. She was perfect. It was a long hard labour. Two days in early labour and one full day in labour. My mam had me walking the streets trying to get labour started. I slept in her bed with her as the contractions took over, and I was terrified. As if the pain was not enough, I vomited every ten minutes the entire labour. I thought it would never end. I have never felt fear like it. My mam never left my side. She held my hand as I pushed Mia into the world. I could never have done it without her. She was my absolute rock. She looked as terrified as me and yet was so strong in her support for me.

When I saw Mia for the first time, I intuitively knew she was the reason I was on this Earth. All my instincts had been right. She was tiny with blonde hair and her grandad Coaches blue eyes. I got to hold her for about five minutes and then the sickness started again so my mam was only delighted to take her. She snuggled her right up to her face and she looked so in love with her. She kissed her little red face, pulled her close to her chest and said 'Hi Mia, I am your Nana and I love you so much already'. It was one of the most beautiful moments of my life. I will never forget witnessing my mam become a nana for the first time. I had not seen her that happy since Coach was alive. She was beaming in between the happy tears. It is one of my favourite memories.

The tea and toast after labour is the nicest thing you can ever have, but they put two fig rolls on the plate beside the toast and the vomiting was off again. I have not eaten a fig roll since and it has been 20 years.

The nurse took us down to a ward and my mam went out to ring all the family. My Aunty Collette had driven us in and was outside too. As the nurse pulled the curtain it was just me and Mia for the first time. I stared at every little bit of her. Her perfect little face, her tiny hands, her scrunched up nose, her perfect little red lips. I had created the most beautiful baby girl. I snuggled her into me and whispered to her 'It's me and you now Mia against the world.' That is how I felt. Our bond was unbreakable. About five minutes later the curtain was pulled back, and there was Toni and Karl waiting to meet their niece. Karl had his camera and was snapping photos. I was only out of the labour ward, but they were obsessed with her from the minute they met her. I have the most gorgeous photo of the four of us with her and I treasure it. We suddenly were a family of five again. She seemed to heal so much heartache for us when she arrived. She brought so much love and hope of new beginnings with her when she entered the world.

I was scared when they all had to leave as it was up to me then, but the nurses were lovely and showed me how to feed her and bathe her. We stayed in the hospital for two nights and then we went home to start our new life together.

My Granny was absolutely obsessed with Mia from the minute I brought her home that first night. She snuggled her as we sat eating, and she sang to her. I never felt alone in that first year. We were so lucky to be surrounded by that much love and support. Toni and I shared a room still, and I was on the bottom bunk with Mia in her Moses basket beside me. Toni luckily slept through all the night feeds. I was 19 doing night feeds while all my friends were out partying, but there was nowhere I would rather have been. I felt like Mia was the reason I was on this earth. Like she had always been here with me. I do not think anyone can prepare you for the level of tiredness when you have your first baby. I felt like I had been hit with a sledgehammer. The night feeds were tough. Mia never slept. She barely napped during the day, and she never cried. It was like she just did not need to sleep. I had no idea if I was doing motherhood right or not. 20 years later I am still working it out. That never changes. I wish someone had told me that back then. Hindsight is a great thing. If I could go back and tell myself one thing about motherhood it would be to trust your instinct over anything or anyone else. You have all the answers you just need to trust yourself more. A hard concept to believe as a teenage mam. People automatically assume you won't cope or you'll struggle because of your age and circumstances. Yet I was a caring and loving mother at 19. I was everything she needed. I didn't give myself enough credit back then.

I adored our time together. I was absolutely obsessed with her. She brought out a side in me I did not know was there. It frightened me how much I loved her. When everyone else was at work we would spend our days together. Every morning at half past ten my granny would take Mia so I could have a shower and get dressed. She would snuggle her 'til about 12 when I had to bribe her to hand her back. My mam would come home after work and head straight for Mia. Toni and Karl did the same. Everyone was obsessed with her. She brought so much joy to the house. My friends loved her, and as the first baby in the group she was spoiled rotten. She became the extra little member in the friend group tagging along everywhere we went. She fitted right in. Anytime we went anywhere they all wanted to have her to themselves for a cuddle. At least until she cried and then it was back to me. My life was so different to theirs and yet for the first time since

I had lost my Dad I was genuinely happy and content. In such a better place mentally and loving being a mother. Mia saved my soul. In lots of ways. She was my new life.

CHAPTER 8

Daniel

I had missed calls from Daniel around this time. Mia was only three weeks old at this stage. We still had not really been in touch since Coach's funeral. I had run into him when I was pregnant a few times as his house was only a few doors up from mine. We had chatted and I remember thinking to myself how much I missed him and our friendship. But life got in the way and we both went different directions. I had not been in touch since I had Mia. My mind was just on her constantly. I was busy trying to figure out how to be a mam, not thinking of anything else. I had spent my pregnancy on Mia trying to heal from a lot of trauma, including the toxic relationship with my ex. I had no interest in ever finding a partner again. In my mind it was me and Mia against the world.

I kept meaning to call Daniel back but having a baby was a full-time job. One day there was a knock on the door. I opened it, and there he was. Just like six years before. Still with those kind eyes, that cute shy smile, and that weird feeling he gave my heart. There was no BMX bike this time. Instead, he had presents for Mia. Before I even got to say hello, he looked straight at me and said, 'Don't you answer your phone?' I held out Mia and said, 'I have been busy Daniel.' Our eyes met and the silence hung in the air for a few seconds.

There always seemed to be something unsaid between us. I could not work it out. It was like he knew everything I was thinking and vice versa. That deep connection was always there. I got such an intense sense that something was going to happen between us I can't explain why. I just knew in my soul he was my person. The timing was not great, was it? That was the running theme in my life. Timing. I knew from the minute I met Dan there was something special about him. That first summer that we hung around together is one of my favourite memories of growing up. We spent countless days with our other group of friends Andrew, Darryl, and Amanda. Daniel had been friends with them since he was small. I was the newbie in the group and yet they made me feel so comfortable as if I had known them for years. After coming from such a horrible time in Loughlinstown it was a lovely feeling to have friends like that. I had truly little anxiety around that time in my life because I was so content. We spent most days together, the four of us.

At 14 I could not really understand my feelings about Dan. It was like our hearts were connected,I had never felt like that before. It was so overpowering it slightly frightened me. I wanted to be around him all the time, yet we constantly bickered. It was as if that is how we communicated. He was so shy and reserved. I was hyper and loud. I would take risks with most things whereas Daniel was always Mr. Sensible. That is what I called him anytime we would bicker. We were total opposites in how we did things. Yet our souls seemed entwined. He was so beyond kind and thoughtful. Every single night he would bring me home on his precious BMX bike. I would of course want to stay out past my curfew, and I would insist I would walk home later, but he always got me home safe and on time. He was so clever too. He would sit and do my science homework for me and try teaching me. I would only be half listening because I am beyond stubborn. It must have worked because I went on to get a B in my Leaving Cert science exam and even my teacher was shocked. Thanks to Dan of course. Up until we were about 17 all of us were inseparable. The group had grown bigger by this time and I was delighted to have so many friends.

I still remember mine and Daniel's first kiss. It was Halloween. I was 16 and we were all betting who could get the most kisses. The things we did to entertain ourselves back then! All the group had ventured off and me and Daniel were left standing under the streetlight, both waiting to see who would make the first mov. After what felt like an eternity, he leaned in to kiss me. My heart was thumping so hard I was convinced he could hear it. I remember thinking how soft his lips were and how I never had felt this way when I had kissed anyone else. The kiss went on for quite a while and I think we both said to each other after, 'what the hell was that?' Something seemed to click between us. I had never felt such a powerful connection. We both always seemed to know what the other one was thinking. It was like we could see into each other's souls. I knew the minute that kiss happened that I was in love with him. I had always been. Fear had pushed it away over the years. Fear of our friendship changing. Daniel was my best friend, so it was confusing to me to feel like that about him. We never spoke about it after that as it was just part of the game. I pushed the feeling away again and tried to forget about it. A few weeks later it was Daniel who introduced me to my first serious boyfriend. One of the lads who had been hanging around with us all summer. I remember him setting me up and he almost seemed annoyed that I was saying yes to this boy. I kept asking him what he thought, and should I go out with him? What I really wanted him to say was 'no, go out with me', but he just said 'yes, sure he likes you and you like him so go for it'. I was half gutted. But I never told Dan how I felt about him either. I was convinced he must know. He must feel it. We did not have effective communication skills at 16. I just told myself I was imagining the feelings and the kiss being what it was weeks before, and left it there.

I was in that relationship for about nine months. I did not really see much of Daniel around that time as this was my first committed relationship, so I spent a lot of my time with the boyfriend. Another not so great relationship. When we split, and I went back to hanging around with the gang, it was like Daniel and I could not stand to be around each other. We constantly bickered to the point that one of us would always storm off home. We could not communicate at all. We would start off well but always end up in a debate, and then not talking to each other. Our friendship had totally changed. When we did call in for him, he would never come out. He always said he had to mind his little sister, or wasn't allowed out. I assumed he just didn't want to be friends around that time as he was doing anything to avoid hanging out with us.

He was super stubborn if he thought he was right, and I am the exact same way so to say we clashed was an understatement. All our friends were convinced we hated each other. Far from it but that is how it came across. We went our separate ways again. I started to go out partying with my friends and he went with his. I would run into him on the odd night out and always feel so sad when I saw him. All I wanted to do was tell him how I really felt but I could not get the words out.

We would catch each other's eye across the room and one of us would get brave after a few drinks, we would chat. Not saying what we really wanted to say and then going our separate ways. When Coach died and I saw him at the funeral it meant the absolute world to me. He always showed up when I needed him. No matter what way we were. He was my person. My safe place in the world and it was like we just could not get it together or be brave enough to say it. I ran into him when I was about seven months pregnant with Mia and we chatted and hung out. I remember being so happy we were back in a good space, but my heart was broken at how it had all worked out. My whole focus was this baby now. I closed it off in my mind as a regret and was grateful to have one of my best friends back in my life.

When Daniel arrived that day to see myself and Mia I was surprised. I don't know why I was, he always showed up in the big moments of my life. He had bought Mia nappies, baby clothes, and so much stuff which I thought was so sweet. He asked to hold Mia and I laughed my head off as he held her like he was holding a football. I showed him how to hold her properly and he never put her down the entire visit. It was bittersweet for me. Watching the boy I had loved since I was 14 holding my newborn baby that I had had with someone else that I did not love. It felt almost cruel to me.

I was going to town that day to register Mia's birth. I had planned to go alone but Daniel offered to come. He knew I had done it all alone so far and wanted to support me. I left Mia with my mam, and we hopped on the bus. We were sitting upstairs when I heard a few of my exes' friends behind us. They started to shout things towards me on the bus. Shouting that I was a slut, who would have a baby with me, look at me already out on a date. Where was the baby I had left her already. It went on for a good while. Constant jeering and shouting abuse at me. I was absolutely devastated. I blinked away tears and tried to ignore them. I had dealt with so much abuse from people when I was pregnant, and I did not deserve any of it. I was so sick of being judged. Sick of feeling ashamed. Daniel took my hand and told me they were absolute idiots, and look at the beautiful baby I had brought into the world. What did they all do with their lives? I really needed that support from him. To hear him be so kind and gentle with me made my heart skip a beat. It showed me again why I was absolutely head over heels in love with him. He always had the kindest and purest soul. I don't know anyone else like him. He is so full of love. He also told them to fuck off, which I was happy about. The entire bus ride I kept wishing things had worked out differently for both of us.

We got to the office to register her, and he asked me if I was going to put my ex on the birth certificate. I had gone through the entire pregnancy alone and Mia was now three weeks old and still no contact. Legally I was not sure where I stood regarding what happened if I put his name on her birth certificate. I was 19 and had no idea what the legal process was. Daniel joked I should put his name down. In my head I said I only wish that was how it had been. I left the fathers side blank. I don't feel he deserved to have his name on the certificate. At that moment in time I was her only parent. I was showing up day in and day out. He didn't show up in any way for her. Nothing was going to make me put his name down.

After the appointment Daniel took me to Eddie Rockets for some food. We sat for ages talking like we were kids again. I did not want the day to end. He walked me to my door and hugged me tightly. Neither of us let go and I could feel his heart thumping against mine. it was still there, that powerful feeling. He told me he would always be there for me and Mia. I knew he meant it. I could see it in his eyes.

I texted him later that night and told him how much I appreciated him and all he had done that day and then I typed 'I wish I could have put your name down. If only things had worked out differently.' I hesitated before hitting the send button. I was shaking. His reply is something I still slag him over all these years later. It said 'no prob, yes ha-ha. talk to you later.' WHAT! Haha talk to you later?! That is it?! I was MORTIFIED, then annoyed, then mortified again. I really thought he was feeling what I was feeling. I blamed the hormones for the vulnerable text and panicked thinking of a reply. It was the most awkward few minutes trying to think what to say. 'Only joking, glad we are back friends. Talk to you later.' I then turned my phone off from the pure panic of it all. What was I thinking?

A week or so later my friend Linsy was turning 21. It was my first night out since having Mia. I was super excited. Me and Daniel were texting constantly. He was going up to the nightclub with the gang and we were going to meet them there later. I had three drinks at Linsy's party, and I was in flying form. I hadn't had a drink since I found out I was pregnant, so they hit quickly, to put it mildly. I ended up disclosing information to Linsy in the toilet about Daniel. The kiss at 16. The constant feelings, the day out at the birth cert office. I blurted out that I was absolutely in love with Daniel Finn, and he felt the same but both of us were frightened. The timing was awful. I went on and on about how it could not work. I have a newborn baby. Eventually Linsy, who was just as drunk as me, shouted 'OMG you and Daniel?! How have you kept that to yourself all these years!' I shouted back that I did not know I was in love with him, even though it was so bloody obvious to me now at that moment. It had always been him. I had let my fear talk me out of ever being brave enough to do anything about it.. Sometimes love is such a powerful feeling that it frightens you. That is how it was for me that entire time. I didn't want to risk losing my best friend.

We both went out to the bar and took a shot to calm our nerves, as if we had just discovered some huge news. We then decided that it would be a great idea to go to the nightclub, and for me to confess my love to Daniel. The wine made me confident, clearly. I would never have done it sober. Hormones and alcohol do not mix well. Who knew? But they gave me the courage to tell him something I had been keeping secret for years!

The whole way up in the taxi I tried to talk myself out of it. I had a three week old baby at home. This was scandalous. I could not say it aloud. Linsey just kept saying 'you have to, you have to', as she told the taxi driver the whole wild love story we had created in our heads in the toilets of her party. He joined in on the hype to be fair to him. He was probably scared of us. I would be too. I sent a text telling Daniel I am on the way, and I had to tell him something big. He didn't reply. I assumed he was dancing or something.

I could not get into the club quickly enough. In my head I had wasted five years not saying anything. No more wasting time. I scanned the crowds, and spotted him across the dance floor with the gang. Then I notice the blonde-haired girl he is talking to. *Eh… What was he doing?* In my drunken head Daniel knew I was in love with him. (Again, I had not said it aloud. I blame the wine.) So why was he talking to that girl and standing so close to her? Before I took even a second to realise how insane it sounded, I marched across the dance floor towards them. I placed myself right between him and this poor girl and looked him dead in the eye and said 'What the hell are you doing? Did you get my text? Who is this?' He looked absolutely stunned, as did the girl (rightly so). He said 'what text?', then took out his phone. There was no message from me. Caught up in all the drama of the taxi ride, I had not hit the send button. Oops.

I told Daniel that I needed to talk to him, then I took him by the hand and led him outside to the smoking area at the back of the night club. I suddenly had lost my wine-induced confidence, and I could not get the words out. So instead, I gave out to him for talking to the girl inside (in my head that was completely reasonable). He kept saying "we're just friends though aren't we, why do you care so much?" I finally said "Well you know how I feel. It's obvious. I thought you felt the same way but clearly not." He looked straight at me and said "So finally you say something." I just shrugged my shoulders and said, "It's too late now anyway." I started to walk off, feeling crushed that I hadn't been able to explain myself properly. My eyes were stinging with tears. I thought I'd blown our friendship, blown everything. But out of the blue, I felt Daniel behind me, his hands on my waist. He spun me around to face him, and he kissed me. Everything around us faded away and in that moment, it was just the two of us standing there. It was the most amazing kiss. I did not want to ever stop kissing him. When we finally did pull away, I could not help myself from saying, "it took you bloody long enough" to which he replied, "yea you too!" We were both as stubborn as each other, both of us afraid of messing our friendship up. We stayed outside for a while just the two of us in this bubble. It felt like no one was even around us. That kiss changed our relationship. I was buzzing with happiness. I had never felt like that before when someone kissed me. So this was what love felt like!

We went back inside the club, and all the gang was in there. We ended up kissing again, to the shock of everyone around us. That night was one of the best nights of my life. I knew from that moment on I could never be without Daniel. I was so deeply in love with him. He really was my person this entire time. It was always going to be him. It just took a different way to get there in the end.

CHAPTER 9

The Three Musketeers

Daniel knew from the beginning that Mia and I came as a package. We didn't get to date like most 19-year-olds. We had a newborn baby tagging along the whole way. We started off the opposite way to all our friends. But it never felt odd or strange, that's what I loved the most about our early days together. It came so naturally to us. It was never even an issue that this baby was going to be there. Daniel slotted into Mia and I's life like he was always there. I had never had a healthy relationship until I started going out with him. He was the first partner to truly love and respect me. There were no mind games, no toxicity, no emotional abuse. It was all so refreshing and terrifying. I kept thinking it was all too good to be true. Surely no man could be this kind and wonderful? So supportive and so loving. Daniel had always treated me so well even as a friend but as a partner he spoils me with so much love and adoration and respect. I never question if he ever loves me. I can feel it in my soul from him just by a look in his eyes. The connection was so powerful that I thought it was only in movies that love felt like that. Still twenty years later I cannot believe how strong our connection is.

Dan used to call us the three musketeers. We did everything together. Mia adored Dan. He did so much with her, and he adored her like any new dad. He stepped into that role so effortlessly, so beautifully. Every day he would come to see us after work. He would call down by five pm and he would have to go home by eight pm. He would always give her her supper and bottle and play with her.

My house was always full, and he was not allowed upstairs. My granny was old school that way, and we did not dare cross her. We would take Mia for ice cream or go for a drive, Dan would help me bathe her or he would spend hours pushing her on the swing so I could sit still, which was great as I was completely exhausted most of the time. He was always trying to help her or to give me a break. He would take her out on little shopping trips. He adored her.

Mia never slept a full night until she was eight years old. She would sit up for hours, hyper, jumping all over the bed. She was obsessed with the Australian kids show Hi-5,and would watch it on repeat. She took about two hours every night to settle to sleep, but by 11 pm she was wide awake again, as if she had slept for 12 hours. I did not realise that wasn't normal. She was my first baby, and I was only 19. I had no idea what to expect with her.

We used to live for the weekends, as Dan's parents had a holiday home in Co Wexford and they would let Mia and I stay in his house while they were away. Some of my favourite memories are those weekends. We had two whole nights a week that we could be a proper little family. My mam, aunties and my moms friends who are like my family would all take turns minding Mia for us on Saturday nights so we could go out with the gang, and we could just be two normal 19-year-olds. We were so lucky with the support we got with Mia. We would take her off every Sunday to a farm or the zoo. Daniel cherished his time with her. He was besotted with her. Our relationship had moved so incredibly fast and yet it all felt so right. I am aware there are not many relationships like ours, and that's why it is so special to me. Daniel chose to take on the role of being Mia's dad, even when people thought he was mad to take on a baby at his age. He gave up his freedom to take on that role when he didn't have to. It made me fall in love with him even more. He was the most natural Dad I had ever seen, and he still is 19 years later.

When we would talk to Mia, we would always call Daniel by his name. We never wanted to force the word 'dad,' but she called him that from the time she was about nine months old. He was her dad. They just did not have the biological component. It was that simple for us. When Mia was a year old, we found a place of our own, and finally we got to be a proper family all the time. We could barely afford it but we were determined to move in together. It was a two bed house in Wicklow in a quiet area. As soon as we went to see it I fell in love with it. Mia would have her own room. It was perfect.

We learnt how to become a family in that house. We were renting and loving life. We had our own space now, it wasn't just weekends together any more. That year together really cemented Daniel and Mia's relationship. He would rush home from work every day to spend time with her, and she thought the world of him. She always wanted him to be the one to put her to bed, and he would spend hours trying to get her to sleep after reading all her stories. If he ever felt the heaviness of the responsibility of raising a baby at 19, he never once said it aloud. He would always say Mia completed us. I felt like I was living in a fairytale that year.

Yet I couldn't help but feel that we were on the verge of losing the family we were building. My ex was lurking in the background of our lives, and he did his best to cause chaos and heartache that entire year when it came to Mia. We were thrown into a long drawn-out court battle.

CHAPTER 10

The Court Battle

I had Mia on my own. I heard nothing from my ex when I was pregnant. The first time I saw him again was when he took me to court to get access and guardianship of Mia. She was around five months old at this time. I was still living at home with my family. I was terrified. I didn't get much notice of the court date and it left me little time to apply for free legal aid. So instead, I paid for a solicitor whose advice was to agree to guardianship and access, as those were his legal rights. It was explained to me in a way that I had no choice but to grant it as a Judge would do it anyway. It took me four months to pay off her bill for a twenty minute hearing. I was young, I hadn't got the first clue about family court. He was granted access to see Mia twice a week, in my house with me present, from six to eight in the evening, and 12-2 in the afternoon. He was also ordered to pay maintenance for Mia every week. My Solicitor had asked for €50. He stated he was not working so the Judge settled on that amount. A tin of baby food alone was €12 twice a week so it wouldn't go very far.

I kept written diaries of every access visit and every maintenance payment. I still remember the first visit when he finally came to see Mia, she was around six months old. My stomach was sick and I was full of anxiety. Mia had only had us around her, so I was especially anxious for her. He arrived 20 minutes late. Not a great start. We sat in the sitting room, and it felt so strange to be handing Mia over to him as she had no idea who he was. She got upset so I tried to explain to him how to hold her and what she liked. Even then she showed signs of major anxiety. She kept putting her arms out to me. It killed me not to immediately take her back, but it was his time, so I persevered. He didn't listen to a word I said the whole time he was there, and he looked at me like he hated me.

I kept a calm and civil exterior for Mia's sake, but inside my blood was boiling. It was the longest hour and a half of my life. His access was a disaster from the start. He would either turn up late or not turn up at all. A minimal amount of times he would send a message to let me know something had come up, but mostly there would be no contact from him, he just wouldn't arrive. It was frustrating because I had to make sure I was home those days, I couldn't make plans, had to make sure I wasn't working, and I'd psyche myself up for the whole thing. I would pace up and down the sitting room waiting for him to visit her. The anxiety would rise up in me as the minutes or hours passed by not knowing if he was going to show. I would feel sick and trembling. I absolutely hated the feeling it gave me. Yet I never said no to a visit. I had to put Mia first and legally I couldn't object. That didn't change how wrong it felt though.

He rarely paid maintenance. It never arrived on time, the rare occasion it was paid. I wrote every payment down, to have a record of it in case I needed it in the future. I tried to be proud and not need his money, even though Mia was his responsibility too, but I would have to give in sometimes. I would text him and say I had no money for baby formula because he hadn't paid that week. He would simply tell me to find it off your family or your boyfriend. He did not care one bit. I can still see myself sitting on my bunk bed counting out coins from my savings jar for a container of formula. I was broken. I didn't want to ask my family or Dan for money, and after I bought the formula I sobbed the entire walk home from the shop pushing Mia in her buggy. I was so humiliated and so angry. I promised myself I would never let myself be in that position again. I felt so livid for Mia. She deserved a father that cared about her and loved her. Not one that got joy from playing mind games and ignoring her needs just to get at me. Mia was not a priority in his mind.

After a couple of months of his (very few) visits, he told me he wanted to take her out of my house. He said he didn't feel comfortable with me there. I always went in and out of the room so he could try to bond with her, but I wouldn't leave them alone for the entire visit. He was a stranger to her. He got bored of her easily and sat on his phone. He didn't even feed her more than once. He couldn't get her to nap and would be enraged if she was napping on his 'time with her'. It was a nightmare. But Mia feeling comfortable and safe was my priority, not how he felt.

I had applied to court to have to have the payments enforced during this time. That really angered him. He hounded me to let his sister meet Mia. She had sent presents down. He threatened me with court again and said that if I didn't agree, he would go for full custody. I didn't feel at all comfortable leaving him alone with Mia, and was worried the court would grant it, so I reluctantly agreed to go to the sisters. If they were going to make a genuine effort with Mia, I wasn't going to stop them from seeing her. I thought if I was civil, we would find some common ground. I went to her house with Mia and met him there. At first I could see she was trying to help her brother show up and try to be responsible but as the visit went on it felt like I was being ganged up on to let the supervised visits happen in her house. They seemed to think it was my fault that Mia hadn't got a bond with him as I was always around. I knew in my soul that was not true, but on the other side of that Mia should have been getting to know him and his family. I agreed that she could pick Mia up for a visit without me there, but that she had to stay and supervise the visit instead.

The first time she offered to drive down and collect her. It was one of the most heartbreaking times of my life with Mia. He arrived at the house and was rude and aggressive in his tone. Mia would not go into the car. She was crying, holding on to me for dear life, and so scared that she was clawing her nails into me. They say children read energy, and she definitely does. His sister then got out of the car and was getting annoyed that Mia wouldn't let go of me. I was upset too and my mam came out to the car to try and calm Mia and me down. I walked into the house hysterically crying. I could not watch her go in that state. My mam would not let Mia go though, she was too distressed. We asked both of them if they would come in and spend time with Mia in her home instead, as it wasn't working how they wanted, but they were just so angry and drove off. I got a horrible text afterwards, saying that it was all my fault, and that he was taking me back to court. He stopped showing up for visits again, and the court date came around for the maintenance hearing. Daniel was working and my mam would mind Mia, so I always had to go alone to court. I would wait on our turn in the hall, for hours, sometimes the whole day until we would be the last called in, and he would either not turn up at all or turn up and beg for mercy, saying that he couldn't afford the maintenance payment. He always made sure to smirk at me, as if he had won something over me. It always seemed to go his way. His payments were reduced to €35 but arrears were added on to be paid. I always felt so powerless on those days. The number of days I wasted at court hearings was too many to count.

None of it seemed to be about the best thing for Mia. It was more to torture me. There were only two more visits after that. On one of the visits we took her to Bray Aquarium. It absolutely killed Daniel dropping us down to meet him, but he did it for Mia. Everything we did was for Mia, no one else. We lived together in Bray at this stage and Daniel was the best dad to Mia. Their bond was unmatched and still is. Daniel still talks about how watching us go to meet him crushed his soul, because both Mia and I both looked so sad. Mia loved the aquarium; but my ex didn't speak to her or to me until the end of it where there was a little ball pit and Mia jumped in. It was the only time I saw him play with her for an entire two minutes. The visits were bizarre.

The last time Mia ever saw him was her last visit to his sister's house. She was about one and a half. I remember it like it was yesterday. I allowed her to go if the sister supervised. I remember Daniel pulling up in the car and dropping us off. He was in the garden sunbathing and did not acknowledge me or Mia. I went inside the house to his sister, who barely acknowledged me. I stood awkwardly trying to settle Mia so I could leave. When I got back into the car I saw Mia standing beside him on the blanket. She was hysterical. He didn't comfort her at all. She ran after the car, screaming for us, so I had to pull in and bring her back. He just sat there. No emotion, nothing. It was one of the hardest things I ever did getting back in the car without her. Daniel and I sobbed in the car the entire way home. It was torture for us leaving her there. It felt so wrong. It was not benefitting her at all. I thought the two hours would never be over to go and collect her and when I finally got back there I found him in one room on his phone. Mia was in another room with his sister. Her face was completely swollen from sobbing, and she looked broken. I will never forgive myself for leaving her there that day, but the access was court ordered and I had been warned if I blocked it, I could end up arrested. Where would that leave Mia? Up to that point I felt like I was helpless, but something shifted in me that day when I collected her. I was done. I picked her up and walked out the door and I never looked back. That was the last time he or his sister ever saw her. I swore to myself that day my daughter was never going to be in an environment where she was not loved or cared for again. Mia couldn't settle at all that night she was in such a state. She was traumatised.

The next day I got the bus into Dublin City Centre into the Library, Mia coming along with me in her buggy, and I began to research guardianship, access and what it all meant. I was determined to have his access and guardianship removed. Every solicitor I contacted laughed and said it would never happen. I kept researching anyway. I found a barrister who I can only describe as my guardian angel. I went into more debt paying her, but I did not care. She fought for me as if Mia was her child. The amount of her own time she put into helping us. She was as determined for Justice for us as I was. Her office was based out in the City Centre so there were constant meetings out there with Mia in her buggy playing away with her dolls oblivious to the serious situation surrounding her. She was amazing at her job and really believed in our case. Her determination and belief of us really got me through some of those very heavy and dark days. We spent months getting our case together. Copies of all the access visits, the missed payments, newspaper articles of his cases in the criminal court, which I had no idea about until I went researching. We took statements from my mam and Daniel about how they had witnessed the stress Mia was put under at visits, and his behaviour around her. At this stage I was owed thousands in missed maintenance payments and arrears, so we filed for a court date about that. I still had not heard anything from him; it was like he had vanished. The court date arrived, and he didn't show up. Finally, the judge took pity on me and ordered a bench warrant for his arrest. Which is rare even now, all these years later. Every day after that for three months I rang the local garda station to see if they had arrested him. I was always told the same thing. They wouldn't just call his house and arrest him over maintenance payments. They didn't seem to be in a position to help. It's a very one step forward ten steps back situation to deal with. There is nowhere to turn and it's up to you to fight it. It was such a frustrating experience. I felt as soon as I got somewhere another door closed in our faces. I would go into the church every single day before I collected Mia from creche, and I would beg and pray for it all to go our way. I felt so broken some days that I struggled to keep up the fight, but I only had to look at Mia and know I had to keep going for her. Eventually he was arrested. He'd done something and been pulled by the garda and when they searched his name, they saw he had a bench warrant out for his arrest. He was sentenced to three months in jail for all the money he owed to Mia. We filed our final court documents to have his guardianship and access removed straight after that.

I will never forget that day. It was just me and my barrister. We brought folder after folder of evidence showing that he was not responsible or trustworthy enough to have those rights over Mia. When you go into family court you must go up to the witness box and speak directly to the judge. I was trembling with anxiety and adrenaline. This was my only shot to protect Mia. She asked me questions and I answered honestly. My barrister put our case to the court and asked me question after question. I could feel his eyes fixed on me, his face full of anger. I just kept picturing Mia.

Then it was his turn to get into the witness box. He stared directly at me and said "Are you ever going to stop fighting me for the maintenance and access?" I stared right through him and said "Never". We held the stare for what felt like an eternity until he uttered the words "Fine I give up my rights to her. I give up everything as long as you don't keep coming for the money that I owe you."

I was stunned. He was willing to give up his rights to Mia over money. Talk about proving my point of how he was not good enough to be in her life. She deserved so much better. I was disgusted by him. All the hell he had put us through, and it came down to this. It was a game to him. He didn't care about her at all. My barrister grabbed my arm and asked what I wanted to do. I took a deep breath in and replied to the court "What I came here to do. Keep my daughter safe. I'll drop the maintenance order if he hands over his rights". The judge asked him if he was sure he knew what he was doing, and he answered yes. I have never felt such relief wash over me.

The feeling of finally being free from his torment and games was wonderful, as was the knowledge that Mia would now be safe growing up in a family that loved and adored her. The battle was over. I got in my car and cried my heart out wishing my dad had been there, then I drove home and gave Mia the biggest cuddle I could between tears. I had done my job as her mother and protected her. She was safe. We never heard from him or saw him again.

Daniel, Mia and I went back to concentrating on the happy life we were building together for the rest of the year after that. We were creating our own family in our own way. The three musketeers navigating family life and everything that came along with it.

We had Mia's second birthday party in the house and all our family and friends came to it. Mia's second birthday will always be bittersweet for me. I was so happy to be celebrating her with Daniel and yet that day haunts me too. We had found out that week that I was about 6 weeks pregnant. It was a shock, it wasn't planned, and no one knew but us. I remember going upstairs as I had awful cramps. I had never had cramps like it. I sat on the toilet, and I miscarried. I was shaking. I went into shock. I sat for a few minutes to try and get myself together. I could hear them laughing and chatting downstairs. I stared into the toilet in disbelief. It was such a strange feeling. I sobbed quietly, cleaned myself up, took a deep breath, and went downstairs as Mia was waiting with her cake. I have a photo of that moment. In it, I have a smile on my face as Dan and I help Mia blow out the candles. No one would have guessed what I had just gone through upstairs. It reminds me how much I have hidden behind a mask a lot of my life. Put a smile on for everyone, do not ruin the day. I certainly did not want Mia's day ruined, so we carried on. I thought the party would never end. The cramps were constant and my heart was broken and yet I was going around in a daze handing out party bags forcing myself to entertain. I didn't want Mia's birthday ruined by me. I kept looking at Daniel who was oblivious to what I was about to tell him. I felt sick thinking of how sad he was going to be.

When the party was over, I told Daniel, and we sobbed together all night long. He was devastated. It seemed extra cruel to happen on Mia's day. Every year on Mia's birthday I always light a candle for the little life that did not make it into our family. I went on to see a medium years later and she told me how I had a son who was sitting on my dad's lap, and he was not meant for this world, so my dad was minding him. It gave me huge comfort as I was so young I instantly blamed myself for the miscarriage. Mediums are not for everyone, but it really helped me heal that part of my life. There is such a stigma around miscarriage, and I wish I had been more open about it back then. I was too worried about being judged as we were still so young.

About six months later I decided to sign up for college and study childcare. The college had a creche that Mia could attend, and I could finally do something for myself. I remember being so excited for a fresh start. We went down to Dan's parent's holiday home for the weekend to celebrate. I woke up on Sunday morning and popped Mia in her highchair so I could make breakfast. As soon as the eggs were cooked, I felt sick. The only time eggs make me feel ill is when I am pregnant. I called Daniel who instantly went so white

I thought he would faint. I sent him to buy three pregnancy tests and I still laugh when I think about him hiding them under his coat walking out of Tesco.

He was sweating buckets. The drama of it all. I took the first test, and it instantly came up positive. I took two more. Yep, pregnant. I called Daniel into the bathroom and held the tests up. He said, "Okay, we will be fine." Then he walked out of the house and sat in the car in the driveway for about a half hour looking shell shocked. I eventually went out and said, "Are you coming back in? We'll figure it out!" That has been our motto for 20 years. We'll figure it out. He came back inside, and eventually the colour returned to his cheeks. We were 22. That is how we found out the three musketeers were going to be a family of four. So much for college. Life had other plans for me!

CHAPTER 11

Along Came Ava

I think the pregnancy with Ava was such a nerve-racking one because we had moved home. Mia and I went to mams and Daniel to his parents house. We would be able to save for a house. So now I was pregnant with a very hyper toddler who still did not sleep great, and I was staying in a box room. It was not ideal. It did, however, push us to find a family home. We saved any spare money we had, which was not a lot. Daniel was in his last year as an apprentice bricklayer. I was working part time in Buy and Sell magazine, and Mia was in creche three days a week eight am to two pm. The creche fee took nearly all of my small wage so it was stressful to say the least. But we made it work like we always did.

I was violently sick during my pregnancy with Ava just like I was Mia. I had constant morning sickness. Twenty-four seven. I spent many days going in and out of hospital to be put on drips to be rehydrated. The difference this time was that I didn't have to do it alone. Daniel was there by my side through all of it. We were so excited. He bought baby books, he bought everything we would need. He worked constantly around his college days, saving for the baby and our future. He came down every night to see us both. I really struggled living separately. It was lonely at times even though my house was full. I wanted us to have our own home again. It felt like we'd had to sacrifice a lot to get together again before this baby arrived. I was sick the entire drive to Mia's creche and my work. I spent about two hours in traffic every morning holding a plastic bag in my lap to retch into. It was hard going. I do not know how I got through those days. I never slept a full night during my pregnancy as I was so anxious about finding a house. Plus, Mia never slept, and I was going through the court battle with my ex over Mia at that time too. The anxiety and low moods were at an all time high. I was struggling mentally and instead of working on that I kept just pushing through. Thinking it was meant to be this hard. We were both fighting so hard to get our own family unit but it was taking a huge toll on us.

There was a lot going on. Being a mother is the one thing in life that has always driven me to keep going. Giving up is not an option. I felt like once I became a mother, I had a reason to be here. We found out we were having another girl, and we picked the name Ava. It means 'life filled with spirit.' It describes Ava perfectly.

Ava Elizabeth Finn was due on the 17th of February 2008. Just like her big sister she decided to arrive late. 12 days later on the 29th of February making her one of the first leap year babies to be born that year. It was decided I was to be induced when I was in my check up 11 days over. Daniel was doing his exams and he ran from college, which was on the other side of town, over to the hospital. . I was induced later that night, and it is still one of my favourite memories of us together. We were up on the pre-labour ward and everyone around me was going into full labour. The shouts and groans were full on, as any woman will tell you in those wards. I was terrified listening to them, probably more than I was with Mia because I now knew what was coming. Ignorance was bliss on my first labour.

This was Daniel's first time, and he was terrified but never showed it. He just focused on me. He kept trying to make me laugh through my early contractions. He would bounce around the bed on my birthing ball, he told me jokes, he would do impressions of the other dads, impressions of me, anything to make me laugh. He was my saviour in those early hours of labour. We kept talking about Ava, wondering who she would look like? Would she have red hair? Dan's dad and sister both had red hair. Would she be tiny? My bump was tiny, so we assumed so. We spoke about how wild it was that we were going to have two kids by 22. How quickly our lives had changed since we got together. We chatted about everything from when we were kids to now being where we were. How we had made what seemed impossible to a reality with our relationship, our family life, everything. It was such a special few hours.

Then the contractions hit hard and there was no more laughing. From one in the morning until five I battled through each contraction. The pain was unbearable, and I finally got an epidural. I thought that would calm my fear and anxiety, but it did not. I started to vomit uncontrollably. My body was shaking as if it was in shock. The fear was taking over me and I was so afraid to be in labour when I felt so weak. I genuinely didn't know if I could push Ava out. I was completely burnt out, exhausted from not sleeping for nine months, raising a toddler, the court battle, and all the stress of Dan and I living apart during my pregancy. I did not realise that at the time though. I just felt like a failure in that labour room. I really struggled to deliver Ava. At one point the doctor gave out to me for not pushing hard enough. More shame piled on. Daniel was my only saving grace. He never let go of my hand. He just kept telling me I could do it and that he knew how strong I was and to push through my fear. I wasn't alone. He was the one who got me through the labour. Finally at 6.35am on the 29th of February, Ava came screaming into the world, with a head full of jet-black hair. So much hair! She was small, like we thought she would be, weighing 5lbs 2oz. But she was beautiful, and so perfect. When they placed her on my chest all the pain disappeared, and it was all worth it. I couldn't stop staring at her. I felt like my heart had doubled in size with love. I could not believe she was finally here.

Daniel took Ava from me and I will never forget the look on his face when he held her for the first time. He was besotted with her. It was really moving for me as I did not have that to share with him with Mia. Daniel gave her a bottle, and she drank all of it, burped, and slept for about five hours after that. She was a dream baby from the get-go.

It had been quite a severe labour, and I had to be fixed up for quite some time. My body was still in shock. I could not stop shaking. I was moved into a really overcrowded ward then, to the point there was not even a curtain to share. I had to sit on a bed pan to go to the toilet and I was vomiting into a bowl at the same time. I couldn't even hold Ava. I was so weak. It was such an embarrassing and low moment. My whole hospital experience was traumatic. When I asked a midwife for help I was told Ava was my second child and to just get on with it . It broke me to be treated like that. There was no support besides Daniel. He stayed as long as he could, and I remember feeling so scared when he left as I had no energy. It frightened me as I never felt like that the first time around. The fear and full blown anxiety took over me. I kept trying to talk myself around but there was no calming me. It all felt so off.

I felt like I was not good enough for Ava being so weak and sick. It makes me incredibly angry 16 years later writing this. My experience was not okay, and it should never have been that way. We deserved better. The whole experience was made so negative by so many people there. But I was so young I said nothing, and that angers me still. It's very clear to me now that I was suffering with prenatal and postnatal depression. The treatment in the hospital was disgusting and made everything harder. We were judged for being young parents in the labour room, hence the horrible attitude from the staff. We were made to feel like having two children by the age of 22 was the worst thing you could do. Especially when they heard that Daniel wasn't Mia's biological father. I can still see the look of judgement on their faces. It made me feel so ashamed in what should have been such a happy and exciting time in our lives.

Mia came to meet her new sister the next day, and Ava had 'brought her a doll and dress up bits', which she loved. She held her baby sister, they were so cute that I couldn't wait to get home so we could finally be a family of four. Ava was a dream baby in the hospital, she only woke once during the night and then went straight back to sleep. I could not sleep at all. I stared at her all night long. I was obsessed with her. Yet that lingering feeling of fear wouldn't lift. . I was overly anxious. I felt detached, like I was stuck watching myself from afar. It frightened me. I had never felt like that before.

Our first night home from the hospital, the four of us stayed together in Dan's house. We moved to our new house down in Wexford the next day, an hour away, where we knew no one and had no family. That was the only way the four of us could live together. We could never afford a house in Dublin. It was far too expensive and there were minimal houses available. Wexford was the only affordable option for us but it was a heavy decision to make that took us away from our support system.

Daniel was only given two days off from college at the time, as he had exams and would not qualify to be a bricklayer if he did not attend. I just wanted to get the girls settled into their new home. My feelings could wait, or so I thought. We moved into that house with no floors, no blinds, no furniture except for a bed and a sofa, and we were broke. We did not care. It was ours.

Daniel did the first night feed so I could sleep. He got up the next morning at 6am and went to college, an hour and a half away. He was devastated leaving us. I cried, Mia cried, and tiny little Ava slept through it all. I felt so alone but knew he had to go. It was his career that fed our family. Each night he would come home, feed Ava, play with Mia, and put furniture together. There didn't seem to be enough hours in the day and it was so full on from the get go. Daniel just kept pushing through to help us get settled. I don't know how he didn't collapse from exhaustion. We were both completely overwhelmed with this new dynamic but we kept going for the girls.

My Mam came down and stayed with us for the first few days and she was my guardian angel. I remember she ran me a bubble bath and I just sat there crying nonstop. I was in so much agony recovering from all the stitches I'd been given after my labour, I could barely walk. I had these overwhelming feelings of guilt then too. I felt guilty that Mia didn't have my full attention any more, that I had to split my time. I felt guilty that I was so afraid now that I had Ava too. I was absolutely terrified about being on my own with the two girls, and I had no idea why. My mind seemed to be constantly in overdrive. I was afraid all the time. It was suffocating me. I felt like I was going crazy. I had to get help.

I went to my public health nurse who swiftly told me I had symptoms of severe postnatal depression, so off I went to my GP. I was given medication for my anxiety and sent on my way. Not once did any medical professional think to say, 'this girl is 22 with two kids, has moved to a new county where she is isolated, her partner has no time off, her mental health is suffering, and maybe she needs support and counselling'. That never happened. It took me a lot of counselling years later to deal with the lack of care and support. There was no empathy at all. It was very much an attitude of 'get on with it'. Bury the anxiety and keep moving.

However, if none of that had happened, I would not be so aware of how important it is to look after your mental health, so it taught me a lot. My only outside support was my mam.

She visited us once a week and she would cook, clean, play with Mia, take Ava, and let me sleep. I would go up to her once a week too, to break the isolation. I had no friends where we now lived as I knew no one. Our house was in a huge housing estate that was being built up so for nine months we only had two neighbours. It was a tough time for us. We would see Dan's side of the family at the weekends, if they were down in their holiday home, but the weekdays were lonely and boring at times. It felt like groundhog day. I had no one to talk to but my two girls, all day every day. In a way I think that is a huge part of why I am so close to my kids. I grew up with them really.

The economy went bust later that year, and Daniel was left without work a lot of the time. The only saving grace out of that was he was home to help with the girls. He did every second night of bottle feeds even when he did have work. He made sure to still be available for Mia and Ava, and for me. Every night we would sit and talk, even for 15 minutes, once the girls had gone to bed. A rule we still have twenty years later. We sat and talked about each other's day. No matter how tired or how busy either of us was. That saved us a lot of the time through the hard years. So many times in those early years we could be in the same room and yet I would miss him. Two children so young took over us. We just seemed to be Mom and Dad all the time, but in those brief moments of catch up, it felt like we remembered we were actually people too. Those are really hard days and I don't think people talk enough about how much having kids can affect your relationship. It can be very lonely for both parents in different ways.

Ava slept through the night from the time she was six weeks old. She was a dream baby. You could take her anywhere. We took her to Spain when she was only nine weeks old with Mia and my mam and sister. She was the happiest little angel the entire trip. She grew into the most girly toddler ever. Everything had to be pink. She would go around the house in her little Disney high heels and handbag at two years old. She would only wear dresses with tights and little pumps. At least one item of clothing always had to be pink. She got her first make up set at three and has been a pro ever since. Anywhere she went, her bag, makeup, and her baby doll had to go. She was so maternal even as a child herself. Always so caring. The running joke in our house was that Ava was so laid back she would not know if you had even left the room. She was always daydreaming or off in her own world. She and Mia played great together, although Ava always acted like she was the big sister to Mia. When Mia would go to school it would just be me and Ava, and I loved that I had that time to bond with her, just the two of us. I have always strived to give her that time. Still to this day I make sure we have that, and 16 years later we could not be closer.

Mia was assessed for Autism when she was three. She was having so many issues at home and in preschool. She was having major meltdowns, she seemed constantly overstimulated.

In preschool she was constantly being described as being in a world of her own and not engaging in any social activity at all. I put it down initially to her adjusting to a new house and baby. I actually kept her in her preschool in Dublin every day and drove up to collect her to minimize her change of routine at the start. It was really tough. We didn't even know what that word meant at the time. It was all new to us. Mia and Ava were completely different as kids, so I did not initially have any concerns about Ava, but when she started primary school, suddenly all the red flags were there, just like they were for Mia. Her preschool said that she did not have a great attention span. She was extremely clumsy, always falling over. She was super fidgety, and when she got hyper there was no getting her back down without an almighty crash. It was suggested quite quickly that she might have ADHD. I had not heard much about ADHD. Back then the stigma was if you were hyper or bold you had ADHD. Something that absolutely boils my blood now. Such an ignorant statement filled with negative language and yet still one I hear a lot. You could not be assessed for ADHD under six years old, so we waited till she turned six. She was anxious daily going to school. Ava cried every single day of her primary school life. It was awful. I used to dread collecting her. She would come out so cranky and so overwhelmed. She had been the easiest-going happy social little girl 'till she was four, and then once she started school it was like her whole nervous system was thrown out of whack.

It is the only way I can describe it. She became extremely sensitive and emotional. She could have 5 mood swings in an hour that's how it felt. I tried everything to help her. Star charts, reward charts, positive reinforcement, parenting courses, joining parenting groups. You name it, I have tried it. My gut told me there was something going on with her. We booked the assessment for Ava, and she was diagnosed with ADHD. I felt relief for her so that she had a reason now to why she was feeling the way she was and for us so we could educate ourselves about it. Ava suffered with severe anxiety and still does. She can manage it alot better now that she is nearly 17 but it really has destroyed her when she is having a bad time with it over the years. It has controlled a lot of her life. When Ava is content and is managing her ADHD she is in amazing form and can soar through life. When she is having a hard time with her moods and anxiety and normal life drama in general she can get very down into a very low space so it is a lifelong battle of minding her mental health over everything. That is her and our number one priority. We tried play therapy for her and it did help when she was younger for quite some time. We also focus on giving her as much time as we could with us both individually. She is a middle child after all on top of living in a neurodivergent home. She needs that from us. She could never fall asleep without being absolutely hysterical out of pure frustration. We would spend hours battling bedtime with her. She was prescribed melatonin but it didn't work for her, so we made the decision to stop battling a strict unrealistic bedtime for someone with ADHD and instead followed her lead of creating her own nighttime routine that she has perfected over the years. I've not woken her for school since first year. She sets her own alarm. She gets up every morning at 630am and does her morning routine including a shower, make-up and hair and her tan. Doing all those steps make her feel set up and ready for the day so we support whatever works for her. She made the decision herself to go on medication for her anxiety this year and attended counselling. She had that space that she needed for herself.

ADHD is a part of who she is, and it causes a lot of issues for her daily. She has a very short social battery, she gets drained easily, her brain constantly feels like there are ten tabs open all at once asking for different things. She procrastinates a lot,She feels very overwhelmed quickly. It's taken a long time for us to learn to help her manage it in a positive and helpful manner. Clear planning, clear instructions on day-to-day life and lots of patience has been the go to for us.It affects her whole life, and I don't think people really see that side to it which is very frustrating for her. It takes an awful lot of mental work for her just to function day to day. Ava's spirit is unmatched. She was born sassy. It's the only way I can describe her. She has picked all her own outfits since age three. She adores makeup and tan. She has been tanning since she was ten. The love that she has for herself truly makes me so proud of her. She is strong, fiery, enthusiastic and knows her worth. Ava has the biggest heart and is one of the kindest people I know. She will not accept any less than she deserves and sets clear boundaries. She is stunningly beautiful inside and out. You will not find a better sister, daughter and friend than her. She adores her family and God help anyone who crosses any of us, she is protective as she is loyal. She is who I would have loved to be if I had been brave enough. She makes me a better person, a better mother. She teaches me daily about life. She has a really wise soul. She sees the world in a brilliantly refreshing way. There is nothing fake about her. Ava is fierce. A wild free spirit. Her vibe is infectious. Ava instantly makes us in a better mood when she is around. She has definitely taught me grace and patience because her stubbornness as a teenager has been on another level some days (the internal screaming in my head has been real!), but I have tried to see it all from her point of view. Growing up in this world with ADHD is beyond tough so I try to give as much grace as I can, but I am still learning daily about my children and their conditions. I try my absolute best everyday to be the mother they need. I don't always get it right, but I never give up trying. Ava is 16 years old now and is everything this world needs. She will absolutely change the world.

CHAPTER 12

Autism, a new world

As I mentioned earlier, Mia never slept. She would sit up for hours, hyper, jumping all over the bed and watching her favourite shows repeatedly. She was very shy around others and stuck to us like glue. She did not seem to cope with any change in routine and as for socialising, it was non-existent. She ate the same thing every day. Pasta and yogurts. That is it. She struggled with anyone even coming by the house. It annoyed her so much. Her meltdowns were extreme. She would go from zero to one hundred in ten seconds. An explosion of different emotions. Any minor change tipped her over the edge. Every day when I collected her from creche there were comments of how she was in a world of her own, she could not interact with the other kids, she would not eat. But there never seemed to be solutions offered, just a dialogue of how hard she was to mind. I was so young having her and she was my first, so I just thought that was normal, how all kids are. I had no other baby to compare her to. I was learning as she was growing . It was all new to me. I do remember thinking quite often surely it shouldn't be *this difficult!*. When I would bring that point up I would just be told that is how children are. They are hard work. My gut instinct didn't agree.

When she was three, we realised that was *not* how all kids are, and we took her to the doctor, who referred her for an autism assessment. We went to the assessment nine months later, and it was a waste of time. They blamed our age, our parenting and said Mia had severe anxiety, and that is all it was. They suggested a parenting course for us and sent us on our way. I left that assessment blaming myself for all of Mia's issues and feeling like the worst mother in the world.

My instinct still told me there was more to it, so I went home and tried to find information online. All the searches kept suggesting she had autism. I didn't even know what that word meant. The more I researched the more it felt like I was reading about Mia. The definition of autism is 'a lifelong developmental disability or difference which relates to how a person communicates and interacts with others, and how they experience the world around them.'

The Māori word for autism is 'Takiwatanga.' Which means 'in his/her own time and space.' That is my favourite definition as it's not filled with negative language. I quickly learnt that the language and research around autism is quite negative. We decided to have Mia assessed privately, as waiting on the public list was going to take years and the research said early intervention is key to access support and services.

The whole assessment process is draining, upsetting and will rip your heart into pieces. It is pages and pages of a checklist of all the things your child cannot do. Never ending questions. Have their milestones been reached? Do they give eye contact? What is their speech like? Are they toilet trained? Do they have angry outbursts? Do they have friends? Good social skills? Communication? Diet? Sleep patterns? Behaviours. It always made me feel so uncomfortable to sit in front of Mia and talk about her so negatively. The language around it is toxic in a lot of ways. There is so much more known about autism now, and that assessment process needs to be scrapped and redone. It is completely outdated. We know so much more now about it that the overhaul of the system is essential.

Autism in girls is harder to diagnose, as girls are more prone to be maskers. Masking is making efforts to manually act in ways that come natural to neurotypical people to meet social expectations and blend into society. However the effects of that lead to autistic burnout and other mental health issues. Something I never even knew was a thing until I learnt about autism. Mia's final diagnosis was Autism, ADHD, Oppositional Defiant Disorder, Dyspraxia, and a general anxiety disorder.

The only word I understood at the time was anxiety disorder, because of my own struggles with anxiety since I was a child. All the others were just words I had never heard before. I remember leaving the assessment feeling relieved that someone had finally put a name to Mia's ways, but also with a feeling of grief in a way, as it all seemed so negative. I was not going to raise the child I had pictured in my mind. You have to grieve for the child you thought you were going to have. Life was not going to be what you had envisioned for them. Everything was going to be so much harder.

Mia was not a 'normal child'. She had this label now. It was a label we needed to access support and services, but still she was different to other kids her age. We had lunch, just the three of us, after the assessment. While Mia coloured, Daniel and I tried to talk about what we had just heard, but in a positive light as Mia was right beside us. We both agreed that Mia was still Mia. She just needed extra help and support. We would not allow ourselves to go down the negative road. Which is extremely easy to do after an assessment like that. Our view on that was, how would it help Mia? She needed us more than ever now. We had to be positive and proactive. There was no other way for us. I honestly believe that attitude is the reason Mia is who she is today. We had that mindset from the minute she was diagnosed.

We drove home in silence, both of us processing the day. It was a lot to process. When we got home, I went into my bathroom and cried for a good half hour. I let it all out. The sadness, the confusion, the guilt I felt that I didn't know about autism, ADHD, all of it. I washed my face, went downstairs, got a paper and pen and started to write down ways we could help Mia. I researched everything. Still to this day I am so glad I chose that approach instead of a negative one. I knew if I had taken the other option we would not be who Mia needed. She needed strong positive people in her corner. She needed to be loved harder on her bad days. She needed cheerleaders and a strong support system. Us having a negative and angry outlook wouldn't allow us to be what she needed.Of course we have our bad moments or our own bad days but that's totally normal. Autism is hard. Loving my kids is not. I never want my children to feel they were a burden to me. It's up to me to process all my own feelings about it so it doesn't affect them. They have enough to deal with. We have to be their safe place.

There were lots of websites that stated you were 'entitled to support and services' but I soon realised they were impossible to access. We were told to link in with the GP and the public health service. That was a disaster from the get-go. They would not accept Mia's private report. They had their own criteria to meet, and she did not meet it. More referrals and more waiting lists. It really felt like taking one step forward and then having to take twelve back. None of it was a straightforward process. I spent most evenings researching, trying to learn all I could about Mia's diagnosis. I attended every course I could find. I went to conferences to hear people speak about autism, how it impacted their lives and how it all turned out. I focused on the positives as much as I could but there is nothing about autism that is easy. It is an extraordinarily complex disability.

No two autistic people are the same. I had to throw myself into Mia's world and I learnt best from her about it. I took a stand early on at the beginning of our Autism journey to listen to Mia first, experts second. If you want to know about autism, ask the autistic person in your life. Learn from them, enter their world, and truly watch and listen. Unless the experts are autistic themselves, their opinions on how we should do certain things never took up space in my head. That's probably because most people we have had to encounter, be it a psychologist, a psychiatrist, or even an autism liaison officer was always a hugely negative experience for us sadly. Unless we went the private route. Something that hit me straight away when Mia was diagnosed was the ignorance around autism. I had no idea people could be so judgemental and so ignorant. Especially the people running the services that are meant to help! It still shocks me all these years later, and it saddens me that nothing has changed. You go to these people desperate for help for your children and they immediately treat you like a villain. That's what it feels like. Your parenting is questioned, your family life. It's like they will do anything not to help so you might just give up and go away. It is the most toxic system to deal with. 20 years of dealing with the public health system and not a lot has progressed. The waiting lists are still years long for basic services. There are not enough Psychologists or psychiatrists to fill the vacant posts. Not enough OTs, no play therapists and barely any social groups for the children and if you do get a place on any therapy, you're usually only entitled to six sessions in that time. Then back to the waiting list for another few years. I think I have heard the sentence 'She doesn't look autistic' at least 300 times in my lifetime. I always respond to that with 'what does autism look like?' That usually stuns the person for a couple of seconds till the awkward silence passes. I do believe our generation is more open to learning and to listening and taking initiative in helping. However, we have a huge battle to go for inclusion. For me as a mother that is the most heartbreaking and soul-destroying part of being a 'different' family. It has kept me up more nights than I can count, crying at the cold and ignorant behaviour of others towards my family. Knowing my children are always at a disadvantage as they try to fit into a world that wasn't built for them. A world made for neurotypical people,not neurodivergent people. It is a bewildering place for neurodiverse people with over-sensitive sensory systems and they battle to process the intense stream of information of daily life. It's like telling a neurotypical person to go live on mars and fit in easily. No questions just figure it out.

When Mia was little her biggest struggles were social skills, anxiety, and her defiance. She really struggled. We did so many therapies. Dan took on extra jobs to help pay for them. Through the health system she got eight Occupational Therapy sessions. She would barely participate. The oppositional defiance disorder was one of the hardest aspects to work with when it came to helping Mia. Daniel and I were the only people to whom she would listen. I would take her to all of her therapy appointments and she would sit there and say nothing. She would constantly look to me to answer for her.

The therapists would try everything to get her to engage with them and she would just stare straight ahead. I can still feel the awkward tension from those early sessions. Torture. I was half embarrassed that she was being so stubborn and defiant, and the other half of me was in awe of her defiance.

She would absolutely not engage with people who she felt were not the right ones to help her. Every therapy appointment we attended, be it OT, social skills, or play therapy, she would say exactly which therapist worked for her. From the time Mia was able to talk she could read adults like I had never seen. It was like she could see right into their soul and tell if they were a good person or not. So much for autistic people not being able to read people's expressions or emotions because this kid had a gift doing it. Still to this day she is spot on with adults and knows if they are a good person or not. The running joke in our family is if Mia wants you in her life, you must be a great person with a good and pure soul. If she doesn't, she will let you know, either with her severe dirty look or her skill of completely blanking you.

God help you if you hurt her. She rarely gives second chances. She takes no prisoners when it comes to setting boundaries of who she wants in her life. Something that took me 38 years to do for myself,she has been doing since she was a toddler. However, that skill stopped short when it came to people her own age. She was extremely vulnerable. She spent her entire school life being bullied,all through primary and secondary school. Horrendously. She could not read other kids at all. She was always so confused by their behaviour. She would cling on to one good friend and that was her safety net. She did years of social skills therapy to help with that. They paired her with one or two other children and they would learn all about social skills and communication. Turn taking, initiating play, solutions to everyday social issues she was having in school. The therapists were amazing with her.

They were based in Enniscorthy and she would attend once a week for two hours. Ava would have to wait around with me as Dan was working and she never complained once. They had dogs there so she would spend her time playing with them or we would play with the toys. Even though all of Mia's reports recommended she have a Special Needs Assistant, she was never given one in primary school, although she had access to resource hours. I used to dread collecting her from school. Every single day she came out hysterically crying, either from being completely overwhelmed by the school environment, or from being bullied. Mia went through three primary schools. I removed her in fourth class from the second one as the bullying was so bad she was having daily meltdowns and threatening to hurt herself. I could not risk her hurting herself. Those meltdowns were some of the scariest moments to witness with Mia. She would be hysterical and screaming in utter desperation. She would claw at her skin as if she could not bear to be in her own body. We could not calm her for hours. Sometimes even days. When she did finally calm down she would go into complete burn out for days after. I felt like a failure that I couldn't fix her pain. She was so distraught. Meltdowns still trigger my own anxiety to this day as it's torturous as a parent to witness. I think that is the side of autism people don't see. It is beyond heartbreaking. There is no controlling it. You try different scenarios hoping that your children don't reach that point. It takes a long time to manage that side of things and you can be the most organised person in the world planning their schedule to a tee, attending therapies , trying every way possible to avoid that scenario and one small thing can set it off. You can't switch off anxiety or autism. So, I decided to homeschool her till we found a school that could work with her and not against her. I gave up my job as an SNA which I was devastated about, but Mia needed me more. Homeschooling was one of the hardest things I have ever done. I set up a timetable for lessons at home, but tried to focus more on life skills, mental health, and academics too. We would go to the library and do projects on things she enjoyed. We kept a happiness diary to keep track of her mental health. Instantly the meltdowns stopped, and as she was home with me all the time she was not being bullied any more.

There were a lot of spinning plates to manage, and it was on me most of the time while Dan worked constantly to ease the financial side of things. We were saving for our wedding at the time, so there was lots of pressure on both me and Daniel to push forward daily. That year parenting was one of my hardest. I was suddenly a teacher, therapist, carer, and mother all rolled into one. My mam still came down once a week to help me, and Daniel went into work late on a Wednesday so I could get out of the house to meet my friends for a much-needed walk and rant. I was given a home support worker two hours a week and Brenda was my lifesaver.. Mia loved her. She even minded our kids at our wedding. I adored her and was so sad when she left after a year. She was not replaced by the health service. I was told my family did not meet the criteria for support. All the services we did access we paid for ourselves. Those bills went high into thousands of euros. Those services included Occupational Therapy, Social Skills therapy, play therapy, equestrian therapy, speech therapy to name a few.

I left no stone unturned. I tried as many things as possible to understand what my children needed. I went into auto pilot for years doing that. The stress and pressure would get to me every couple of months but I always found a way to keep going. They needed me. Mia started a new school for fifth class, and it was a two hour journey on the bus each morning and evening. It took its toll on her, so for two years I would drive down towards the new school and meet the bus so she was home a bit earlier. It took a lot of work to get Mia through school life, especially when it felt like I was the one doing it all, except for the help of an amazing resource teacher in her new school. He was a guardian angel to her and us. He worked so hard with her. He encouraged her so much and always made her feel like she belonged just as much as the other kids. She just had to learn differently. There is no way she would have gotten through those two years of primary school without him. He believed in her and never saw her disabilities as a negative thing. He learned to teach her in the way she needed. That is a rare gift that not many have and we will always be so grateful to him.

Secondary school was hell from the first day for Mia. I did not think she would make it out alive some days. She was bullied every single day. Those days were the scariest. Not knowing if the bullying would tip her over the edge. The school was supportive and did step in as much as they could, but kids are cruel and find ways. We confronted the bullies, which actually made it worse, but parents will try anything to keep their children safe. I am very protective, and I become the fiercest version of myself if someone has hurt my children. The bullies eventually backed away, but Mia had to put up with years of that behaviour.

Mia got access to the autism unit in secondary school and an SNA, and had wonderful teachers to help her. They worked on so many things with her including social skills and academics. She was given an exemption from Irish and Spanish as in 2017 she was diagnosed with a mild learning disability on top of everything else. That explained why she found the academic side of school so tough going too. I always tried my best at home to communicate with the school, and they did the same for us. I never allowed any disability to be used as an escape clause for bad behaviour, cheekiness, anything. She had to learn the hard way like most kids her age when it came to getting into trouble in school for various things. By fifth and sixth year she was constantly mitching off, she could not stand the school environment. She got detention, I grounded her for it. There was always a consequence, autism or not. But she never fitted in and it really destroyed her in so many ways. She never gave up though, and found her circle of friends finally in sixth year. Her people who understand her and love her for who she is. She had to wait an exceptionally long time for true friendship, and she went through hell to find it. Our motto is we do not give up. Especially on the bad days. We cry, we scream, and we feel sorry for ourselves but then we push forward. We deserve to fight for ourselves.

My kids are my reason for being here. Autism and ADHD were always a part of our world, we just did not know it at the beginning. Our whole lives are built around it now. Our approach around it is whatever works best for us as a family. That might not work for others, and that is fine for other people. For us it works. I spent years justifying how I raise my children and why we do things so differently to the 'norm.' It was really refreshing to stop explaining everything, like a weight had been lifted. Sometimes as teen parents you look to outside people for support, agreement, or their opinion, just because you might think you are too young to know the answers. Whereas I have always chosen to listen to my instinct and it has never been wrong. I also listen to my children and their thoughts and opinions. I value theirs more than anyone else's. They are the ones that know the most about their own conditions. They live with them daily.

CHAPTER 13

Along Came Jack

Jack Daniel Finn arrived late, just like his two big sisters. I was induced 12 days after my due date, and at 09.50am on the 29th of September 2011 Jack came into the world weighing 8 lbs 9 ounces after only a four-hour labour. He was perfect. When I placed him on my chest, he felt so big compared to the two girls. I was absolutely over the moon to have a boy. I had been convinced I was going to have three girls. He was my biggest baby and the easiest labour of the three. The only one I had no pain relief on, or an epidural. I had approached pregnancy and labour completely differently this time around. I listened to hypnobirthing videos. Those videos got me through the labour. I minded my mental health a bit more as I really didn't want to get postnatal depression again. The labour was so intense, but I had the best midwife called Andrew who really encouraged me with my breathing and pushing. It was a much more positive environment than my deliveries in Dublin. It was actually a calm labour. Daniel was joking around trying to use the gas and air while I would go into myself with each contraction. I tried the gas and air and hated it. My midwife really encouraged me to follow my instincts with every contraction. I had no epidural this time either as I didn't want to be sick. Daniel was sitting at one stage eating a roast dinner while I powered through the pains. Men and their priorities! Am I right ladies? Besides the dinner break he never let go of my hand encouraging me the entire labour and spraying water on my face. That spray was like a piece of heaven . I helped deliver Jack which was an amazing but very surreal experience.It was really special to me to be able to do that. To reach down and help him out into the world. I felt a huge rush of emotion at that moment. The love I felt in my heart for this gorgeous baby boy. He was perfect. I was 26 years old having Jack and we now had a seven-year-old, a three-and-a-half-year-old and a newborn.

Mia and Ava were so excited to meet Jack. Ava immediately took over with him. She acted like his second mum from day one. She adored him. She would constantly hold him, feed him, and cuddle him to sleep. Mia adored him too and was such a good helper to me with the younger two. She was like my little assistant. We were all besotted with him. We would just constantly cuddle him. He had completed our family.

Daniel and I never put him down. He was our last baby and we wanted to relish every newborn cuddle, take in every inch of him. Jack slotted into our family as if he had always been there. We got to enjoy those early days with him as we had no stress of houses and exam deadlines. It was such a special time as we all adjusted to now being a family of five. Daniel was able to take a week off this time which was brilliant, and he did every second night of night feeds just like he had on Ava the entire time. Jack had colic, and from five pm every day to eight pm he screamed the house down. There was no settling him. They were the hardest hours of the day. It was like he couldn't take a bottle properly. We ended up switching him to a dairy free food at six months because his skin was so bad with eczema, and it was like the food just didn't agree with him. He was not a great sleeper, just like his big sister he didn't need naps or much sleep at night. He could never settle unless he was in our arms or lying on our chest. He constantly moved and grunted in his moses basket or cot and always seemed to be nearly wriggling around in pain. The doctor put it down to the colic but I knew in my heart there was more to it.

When he was a year old it was obvious to me that he was autistic. He didn't sleep, he didn't eat, he clung to me all the time. He was full of anxiety. He didn't seem to react much when people came over to him. He didn't really make eye contact. He wouldn't really settle with anyone else. It was like I was his safe space and he settled best with me, yet he didn't seem to like affection. He rarely hugged anyone. He did not have any interest in the baby toys, the play mats nothing. He never played with toys even as he got older, no matter how much we tried. We even built a sensory room and filled it with toys, board games, jigsaws. He was terrified of certain noises, hair dryers and hand dryers being a big one. His language was very delayed. He just pointed at everything. I saw a lot of Mia's characteristics in him. I put him into creche three mornings a week to help his social skills and his language skills. He screamed when I dropped him off, and when I would collect him, he was always alone crying. It broke my heart. He seemed genuinely traumatised when I would leave or arrive.

He had no interest in anything but painting. The staff at his creche didn't seem to think he was autistic, but again I do believe that comes down to lack of knowledge and training. I knew in my deepest instinct he was. I had lived through it all with Mia, yet I was questioned and doubted daily. It really hurt me. It is extremely draining constantly trying to prove to others, especially those in the education and health system, that you know your child best. A mother's instinct never lies. It is the strongest tool we have when it comes to helping our children, and something I always listen to. Autism has such a stigma attached and not a lot has changed in the past 20 years. That makes me sad for my children. It is much more diagnosed now and yet the education and training still are not there. It baffles me. Jack was diagnosed as autistic when he was nearly three. Privately, as he would be years waiting for a diagnosis publicly. I felt relieved and yet sad when we first heard Jack's diagnosis. I knew from going through everything with Mia we had a huge battle on our hands and to be honest I didn't know if I had the strength a second time around to fight. I felt sad for Jack because everything was going to be so much harder for him than a neurotypical child. No parent wants their children to have to be battling for the most basic human rights but with autism and ADHD too that is how it is. The simplest of tasks are now automatically harder because your brain is wired differently and you're having to grow in a world that is not designed for you.

I immediately started Jack in private speech therapy, occupational therapy, and covered my house in visual aids. Every euro I had went to all my kid's therapies. Daniel was working two jobs, even driving hours to Cork to deliver medical supplies after working a twelve-hour day. It was tough going for both of us, but our kids needed those therapies. I would print out the daily routine, the pictures of where we were going on any day, I would bring pictures into the supermarket of the shopping we were getting, and hand them to him in the hope he would be able to say the words. I used social stories to try preparing him better for change in routine. You name it I have tried it. I don't leave any stone unturned. I have researched so many articles and joined support groups. I have read countless books from authors who are autistic themselves or have worked with autistic children. I wanted to learn more about how my children's brain works and how they see the world. Anything I can do to help them I will. I have attended numerous courses including parenting ones to learn more about how we can accommodate their needs.

I also moved Jack out of his creche/ preschool and into an autism unit preschool. He could access huge resources there; he had a shared special needs assistant, and they understood him. It was the best decision I ever made. Certain staff members looked at me like I was mad when I told them he was moving to a preschool set up for kids that were autistic. I'll never forget how they tried to shame me into not moving him. I heard the whispers; I saw the dirty looks and I heard the comments that it was 'all in my head' from certain people.

It was that very treatment that spurred me on to do what was best for my children. I know them best, I know what they need. That kind of treatment and judgement was never going to be allowed around my children. That goes for anyone in their lives.I will not have people around them who don't make any effort to get to know them truly, that don't accept them for who they are and who have no interest in learning about them. That negative ignorant energy cannot be around them. The damage that kind of attitude does is indescribable, yet it's everywhere. I won't have them feeling ashamed just because their brains are wired differently and they don't follow the crowd. It makes me fight even harder for them. I took the anger I felt, and I used it to help all my children instead of letting it destroy us over the years. The ignorance is always there. It's what you do with it that matters.

When Mia was going through her initial assessments, I didn't speak up at first when there was a rude or nasty comment. It takes a lot of courage to go against the norm in those meetings. You are in with the 'experts', you are a young parent and you do feel slightly overpowered. However, I found my voice after only a few of those encounters. I understood Autism and ADHD more as the years went on, and I started to speak up in all of the kids appointments. For a long time I felt I was going to battle with teachers who had no idea what autism was, and dealing with a failing health system that had no support, just lots of paperwork, years of waiting lists and ignorance. It was, and still is, exhausting. The fight goes on. There is no end in sight. No magical solution. You conquer one issue and then others arise. I have a good rapport now with the children's teachers because I have been open and honest from the beginning and they know I do my part for them, and so do they. They want to see my children succeed and they fight for the support just as much. There will always be a few that are uninformed and don't want to help. They aren't the right fit for your children, but they can also create havoc in those important formative years, as your child's education is in their hands. It's an awful place to be in. The health system is diabolical to deal with and that is putting it generously. Years of waiting lists, not enough staff, not much understanding of autism or ADHD. We went to battle with them for numerous years with not much to show for it.

Jack thrived so much in his preschool unit, and got so much support and services. He had amazing teaching staff and special needs assistants. . He had access to a sensory room whenever it was needed. There were only five other kids in his class and he was able to thrive in that small environment. His speech came on so much, as did his social skills. They worked hard on his emotions too. He had access to occupational therapy. It was probably the only year of his entire school life that I didn't worry about him, as I knew he was getting all that he needed. I got my first hug from Jack in that preschool. That made it all worth it to me. He hugged me for thirty seconds and it still makes me tear up thinking of it as it was the start of him showing affection after so long. It was magical for me. To this day I still get a hug every bedtime and he tells me he loves me at least twice a day. How lucky am I to have that in my life? He came on so much that he was moved into the mainstream school for Junior Infants. We assumed, as he had been in the unit, he would have access to a Special Needs Assistant, but it was denied as he did not have medical issues. Both Mia and Jack's reports state they need an SNA, but one was not granted in primary school to either of them.

The system is so hard to deal with. So much red tape. One step forward, five steps back. That is how I would describe the whole autism services area even now, 20 years later. Moving to mainstream Junior Infants was the beginning of the absolute disaster that has been Jack's school experience. He struggled instantly in the big class setting, he would not settle in school and would cry for me for about an hour after the day started. He had one friend who was just so good to him, but he found it really overwhelming to mix in the class and the yard. The noise, the crowds, the absolute over-stimulation of the entire day. He didn't have much help. He had a very understanding teacher in Junior Infants but no other support. It was a huge difference from the unit, and a real shock to the system for him. Ava was struggling majorly in school too and was getting no support at all for her ADHD. I moved him and Ava to a different primary school in the hope that they would get better help. It didn't work out that way. They both majorly struggled. Ava came out crying most days. Her anxiety really took over her days. She struggled so much with it. They both had access to small class breaks and initially they had resource hours to help with the struggles they were having. Jack lost his resource hours in 4th class as he was 'doing so well'. He never regained them no matter how much I asked. Again, we were told children with autism are entitled to four and a half resource hours a week but yet again that was denied when we tried to access it. He really suffered without those supports to the point it became a daily battle to get him into school. He just about makes it to every midterm break or summer holidays but suffers huge autistic burnout from the stress of all. This leaves him feeling exhausted, depressed, confused, and fed up – and riddled with anxiety. Mia was the exact same. There was no support for Ava for her ADHD at all. It is always a battle for the bare minimum for them. It is a hard pill to swallow knowing you are trying and fighting your best but still not really getting even the basics.

It got to the stage in fourth class that I removed Jack from school two weeks earlier than they finish for summer holidays. For his own mental health. I did the same in fifth class and this year I removed him from school at the end of April. He was being failed by them. So, I had to step in and homeschool him just like I had Mia for the last two months of the school year. We focused more on life skills than academics. I saw a huge change in him instantly. It was like a weight had been lifted off him. The anxiety eased; the meltdowns stopped. He slept and ate better. The anxiety and the lack of support has on him is just too high of a cost to his mental health, so I don't feel we had much choice but to keep him home. It's the reality of living in the autism world. If you live in it, you'll understand that statement immediately. If you don't you have a lot more privilege than you know. Ever hear the saying 'ignorance is bliss?' It couldn't be more accurate! Jack is one of the most intelligent people I know. His soul is so pure. He is so kind and so loving. He is so thoughtful and respectful. He adores animals. We call him the dog whisperer in our house as he is so in sync with them. We have four dogs, two rabbits and four chickens because Jack's passion is animals. We try to encourage his passion or hobbies in any way we can. He adores movie days so once a week I get us cinema popcorn and we watch his choice of movie in his safe place with just us. I found it was a great way to connect with Jack as he doesn't play with toys or build Lego. He doesn't enjoy going to busy places or loud places. He finds social gatherings even with family very hard to cope with. He is happiest at home with us so everything we do with Jack is built around home.

He loves to bake. So, for 12 years our way into Jack's world has been baking and movies and animals. His eyes light up, he is engaged in conversation and his body relaxes, free from the otherwise constant presence of anxiety. The baking and cooking teach him good independence skills too. He has one or two friends in school, but he goes through phases of wanting to socialise. I have spent the entire twelve years trying anything I could to get Jack out and about and mixing. I've had so many playdates, sleepovers, days out, anything I could think of.. But I sat back one day and saw how uncomfortable he was, and I asked him straight out if he enjoyed these forced get-togethers. He did not. He enjoyed the playdates when they were short and sweet. He did enjoy the sleepover with a friend but now he's back to not wanting that either. Who was I helping, with all my great intentions? Certainly not Jack. It made him miserable. I took a step back and followed Jack's lead. I started to listen to him. Truly listen. I think sometimes as the mother it hurts you more than it hurts your child seeing them be so misunderstood. Jack has only ever been invited to one birthday party his entire school life. The year he moved to his new primary school I invited the entire class to his party. I thought it would really help him socially. They all came, and they had a ball as did Jack, or so I thought. Till we got home, and he cried saying he found it all so overwhelming, it burnt him out and he didn't enjoy it. He never got an invite back to any of the parties being held. That broke my heart for him. I cannot understand how they don't see what we see with Jack. The most amazing kid. It was then I learned to stop trying to make Jack fit in. Although he probably would have said no to the invite, he still wants to be thought of. Included, accepted. Especially by his peers. That is the bittersweet and complicated side of being autistic. You want to be included and accepted but you also don't know if you can go out of your comfort zone to do the social thing. It's exhausting and challenging and hard for neurotypical people to get. I think that is why we are very much Jack's friends as well as his family. We are his whole world. I want that world for him to be so accepting and so positive and for him to thrive as the person he is. It only takes small efforts with Jack. He loves when my mam brings him to Costa as she always gets him the drink and crisps he likes. They'll drive straight home but it doesn't matter as she has made the effort with him to do something that makes him feel comfortable. Ava will bake with him, play Uno for hours, or Mia will play the PlayStation as he is a gamer kid and that's where he socialises best and feels most comfortable. Dan will do anything he wants to do so they can connect in their way. Trips to the forest usually with the dogs and an ice cream. Card games for hours. Throwing paper airplanes at each other in the hall. My sister and her husband once camped in their garden with Jack because he was obsessed with camping for a while. It's those small efforts that mean the most.

It's only when I take my own nieces or nephews or my godson out, I see how different our world is to theirs. I try to give them my time as much as possible as being an auntie/godmother is important to me. I know too well having older kids now that the time they want to spend with you is limited. You won't be the cool one for too long! I adore them. They'll tell me all about the clubs they are in, playdates, party invites, their friends, and of course I'm always thrilled for them, yet I have lost count of how many times I have gone home and cried for Jack, and for us sometimes, because that isn't our life. It hurts, and that's totally normal. The other side of that is I adore the life we have. I wouldn't change it. Our whole family has been created around Autism and ADHD. It's okay to feel sad for the life you thought you and your kids were going to have, but don't stay in that mind frame. That's how your mental health gets affected. Feel the loss, grieve it, but don't stay there. I love the life we have worked so hard to create.

I love how unique our family of five is. It is filled with love, inclusion, understanding, and open minds. It is rare, what we have. We have fought very hard to build the family and life that we have together. We are resilient as we are stubborn. That has got us through the hardest days. Being a mother to my three has been the greatest honour. It is a role I have cherished and worked hard at. They deserve the best and nothing less. In all aspects of life. I am so glad I had them young as I grew up alongside them. The five of us have a connection like no other and that alone blurs out the hard days. There have been so many amazing, fun-filled, laugh out loud till your stomach hurts days. I hope my children remember those days when they grow up and think back on their childhood, and not the days where I was tired and short tempered. I hope they know that everyday we give it our all. I hope they felt loved and understood. We try to be all that they deserve. They are my greatest accomplishment in life.

CHAPTER 14

Being Different

As I said in the first chapter, I always felt different and that led to me feeling lonely a lot of times in my life. Those two emotions have always co-existed together for me. I felt lonely in primary school when I was being bullied, I felt it going through losing Dad, and I felt it going through my pregnancy with Mia. I have always felt it. Motherhood, especially Special needs Motherhood is an isolating place. I have had quite a few people throughout my life that have left me feeling so isolated and sad, and as if I am a bad person because I am not like them. From school bullies to ex-partners to people that I still see to this day. I got really good at reading people's facial expressions and body language when I was young because I struggled so much with verbal communication. It's what helped turn me into a chronic people pleaser which I never realised till I started counselling much later in life at 20. By then I had years of experience in how to handle your emotions correctly. I think it's why I can read my own children so much because I know exactly what 'being different entails' and the negativity that can come with it.

I had tried counseling numerous times over the years. My first time with a counsellor was when I had Mia. She fell asleep as I spoke. Full on snoring. Safe to say that put me off for many years. In my head she fell asleep because my story was so boring and not worthy of a session. She was probably just exhausted, but it made me feel awful. I never went back to her.

Instead I destroyed myself mentally for another few years, wondering what was actually wrong with me. Why couldn't I get my emotions together like everyone else I knew. I went to counseling again around 2012. Luckily this time I found the right person. Nigel was my counsellor on and off until August 2024. The last time before this year was in 2021 when I saw him. I would take big breaks in between. I went back this year for two top up sessions after a particularly emotionally hard year . He helped me in so many ways. I owe him a lot. He completely changed my way of thinking and made me realise there was never anything wrong with me. I was different. For many reasons. Trauma being one of them. Cognitive Behavioral Therapy genuinely saved my life. I would attend for months at a time and then take breaks and go back when

I felt I needed it. I would dread going to each session, panic the day of it and think of any excuse not to go but always pushed through as afterwards I felt so much better. I really didn't start looking after my own mental health properly till then. I was so busy being a mother since I was nineteen that I never actually learned the skill to put myself first. I had always suffered with anxiety and my mental health but had never taken the time to truly investigate it.

I thought my counseling would be all about my dad dying, but that was just the beginning of a long list of things over the years. I had no idea how anxiety had controlled my life or the traumas that went with it. Being bullied had left scars. Deep ones. Feeling different and not quite like I belonged had also left extensive damage. How people have treated me over the years has destroyed my self esteem. I felt very broken at times. I've had multiple people be so openly cruel to me over the years. I know in my soul I am a kind and loving person and I didn't deserve any of that. I also know I am not perfect and I have my own faults. I am stubborn, defiant at times and I am fierce when it comes to my children and Husband. I am every inch of a mamma bear or tiger. I also know that that side of me comes from love and a pure heart. I rarely show my temper unless someone hurts my family. However, I have continuously worked through my own issues. Communication being a huge one, setting boundaries and cutting people pleasing ways. A hard habit to break when you've spent your entire life not even knowing what a boundary was. I never back away from trying to improve, learn, and grow. I have had to drag myself out of a lot of dark places when it comes to my mental health. I didn't share that side a lot with my family, until recently. So much stigma and shame resides around mental health. That's something I broke, raising my own children. Mental health comes first. Shame creates a toxic lifestyle, and it is not allowed in our house. My anxiety led to me trying to fix all Mia's issues, including the bullying in her life, just like my dad had tried for me. It's natural for a parent to do that, but I learnt in counseling that if you keep trying to control and fix everything how will your children learn those skills for themselves? I thought that was my role as her mother but I was doing more damage than good. I learnt you can be supportive in the right ways, without overstepping the mark. Listen to your kids. Truly listen. Nine times out of ten they don't want your advice. They just want a supportive ear. Especially listen to the small things, because if you take that time to stop and give them your attention as they get older, they will tell you all the big things. Trust me when they are teens you are going to need the most patience and non-judgemental approach if you want to survive those years. They will humble you like nothing else. Wine helps. So does taking regular breaks from them. Admitting parenthood is hard really helps. Also showing your children that you're a person too, not just a parent. Showing that you have hard days too. That sometimes you're sad or anxious. When my kids were little I always put a mask on for them, as if I always had it together. But how could they learn to work on their own emotions if I was always hiding mine? We all grow up together. It's so important they know that. Children want two things from you. Your time and your love. It really is that simple, but we complicate it and make it so much harder when we let the outside world and their opinions in. Also, generational habits are difficult to break. You're not parenting like your own parents because you are raising a whole new generation in a completely different world to the one you grew up in. Times change. You want to raise good kids? Do the work on yourself. Daily. For life. You owe yourself and your children a happy, healed version of you. Ask your kids their opinions on whatever the situation is that they are struggling with and how they think it can be managed. I learnt all that in years of peeling back layers I didn't even know needed to be peeled. Your children don't want your advice or 'your way of doing it'. They want a listening attentive parent to support them and show love even harder on those hard days. This can be a real struggle when you're all having a hard day. There is no way around it. Parenting is the hardest job going. The good news is, the hard days don't last forever. Good days will follow.

Counselling really changed my parenting style with all three kids. I also learnt that I was trying to control everything around me because of how my dad had died. I had no control over that awful day when he died suddenly. My coping mechanism became obsessively trying to fix everything and everyone around me so they wouldn't feel the hurt I had. Grief is a very complex emotion to go through. I realised it had made my anxiety ten times worse. I also learnt that because I had Mia so young I always felt like I had brought so much shame to my family, and that turned me into even more of a chronic people pleaser. I never wanted to let anyone down again. No matter the cost to my own mental health. It also made me realise just how much trauma I had been through at such a young age. It was bound to leave scars. I should have dealt with my grief years before, but it took me 15 years to process it. It took me up until 2020 to learn how to forgive myself for things that were out of my control. I realised I didn't treat myself very nicely, and that's why I had let people treat me badly. I had no boundaries either. I was keeping the peace constantly – but for who? Certainly not me. It destroyed my mental health. I deserved and still deserve better. I had to learn to love myself and heal my own wounds.

The self-work never stops. I have spent the last four years learning who I am other than 'Mam'. I dedicated my whole life the last 19 years to that role and forgot about who 'Carrie' was in the process. My children are my greatest achievements in life but now they are 19,16 and 13 it is time to bring myself back to life. I had to go back and reclaim the girl I was before I had kids. I owe her that. It's something I still must work on daily. I am my own worst critic. I am slowly realising mom guilt is toxic and damaging, and a waste of precious time. I know deep in my soul I am a great mother to my children. I have given them as much as I can and I will continue to do that, but now I can also give myself some of that love and attention without feeling guilty.

I decided in 2022 that I wanted to be assessed for Autism. As I watched my kids grow up, I slowly realised I saw a lot of myself in them. It had never occurred to me that I too could be autistic. I cancelled the assessment twice. The fear got the better of me but as I continued my healing journey the instinct screaming at me to be assessed would not go away. It was the final piece in my own journey that was missing. So finally, in 2024, I went for my assessment. After numerous sessions and intense questions, surveys, and interviews with no stone left unturned, I was officially diagnosed as autistic on the 11th of March, 2024. I really was my children. I felt instant relief, finally knowing the reason for feeling and seeing things as I did. I felt validated as a person. There was nothing wrong with me. My brain really is wired differently to neurotypical people and knowing that helped heal a lot of my emotional scars. I grew up in a world that wasn't set up for me. Of course I was going to struggle. There were barriers at every turn. I did my best figuring out my place in a very confusing world. I didn't deserve any of the bullying, the horrible treatment over the years from people just because I didn't fit in their box. It was so freeing and healing for me to be diagnosed.

I went through some grief and anger after the initial relief stage. I was angry for all I missed out on, and how I had been treated at times for feeling different. If I had known that I was autistic from when I was little maybe things wouldn't always have been so hard and confusing to deal with. I made peace with it though as back then we had never even heard the word autism.

It was only when I had Mia that it opened that world for me. I am forever grateful for that. Knowing that I am autistic has really helped me set boundaries too. I used to say yes to helping everyone and running myself into the ground. I would go places I didn't want to go as I would feel so uncomfortable, and then be upset for days after. I was constantly damaging myself for people that didn't contribute to mine or my kids' lives. Now I just won't allow that energy into my life. If I don't want to go, I won't. If you don't understand us, our children and their needs, and don't make any effort, you are not welcome in my life. That is my boundary. Life is too short to allow people to add misery and ignorance to it. I wasted so much time looking for validation and understanding in the wrong places. It has destroyed me many times. It's left scars that I have to deal with. I only want to be surrounded by people who genuinely care and understand us. It took me 38 years to finally put myself first in all aspects of my life, and being diagnosed was the last piece of my mental health journey for me. In all aspects of my life. Life was draining before my diagnosis. Now it's peaceful and freeing. It is priceless. Being autistic myself is why I can read my children so well. It's why our souls and hearts are connected. The bond we have is the best feeling in the world. I was meant to teach them and yet they have taught me everything that is important in life. I want my children to have a positive role model. The world needs more of them. We can't expect our children to accept themselves if we are not doing it as their parents. I never want them to feel the loneliness I felt. I want them to see the positives to being neurodivergent. The language around it needs to change rapidly. It is surrounded in so much negativity, and while there are negative aspects, there are so many positive ones too. Loving, kind, pure, honest, unique, passionate and loyal, to name just a few.

There is a statement in my diagnosis report that has stuck with me and It is how I really think the world should look at autism. It goes like this:

'Although it is no surprise to you, I can confirm after these investigations that you are autistic and meet criteria for autism as per the DSM-5-TR and ICD 11. I congratulate you on being part of a community of wonderful people. I hope this is an important part of your journey of self-love and understanding. As you know, autism is not an intellectual disability or a mental illness. Although autism is sometimes described as a disorder and in a neurotypically designed world, being autistic can involve additional challenges when the right supports, and environmental modifications made to make the environment

accessible for autistic people are not in place. Autism is a different neurotype and a valid way to be in this world. People with different neurotypes can find it difficult to understand the perspectives of those who have different neurotypes to theirs. Neurotypical people sometimes do not understand Autistic ways of communicating and interacting and Autistic people do not always understand neurotypical ways of communicating and interacting. There is a growing body of research to indicate that autistic people have far fewer issues understanding and communicating with each other, and that many of the communication issues between autistic and neurotypical people are caused by the neurotypical person (e.g., when they do not wait long enough for a response, or they are not honest). Being autistic means that you experience the world differently to most, and you need extra support in some areas because most of the environments in which you live, and work have been designed to be acceptable and accessible only for neurotypical people and contain neurotypical expectations of how to behave and communicate (for example expectations around eye contact and responding quickly to instructions). I hope that you have found the assessment process useful and that it will be the start of you gaining the support you need in your personal life.'

CHAPTER 15

Time for the Truth

It has taken me over nineteen years to write this book. I am finally writing it now because I have my husband and my children's blessing. It is our story. I want them to know why we had to protect them like we did. I want them to know we never gave up on them. I also wanted to write it for myself. I feel like I owe 19-year-old me this book. We made it through the biggest storm of them all. I want to be able to look back and realise how strong and brave I was on the days where I was my own worst critic. It has taken this long because this chapter of the book is what my entire family life was built around, and my children never knew any of it. Every single day for eighteen years we carried a secret that I honestly thought would rip my family life apart. I woke up every day filled with fear and anxiety wondering was this the day my kids would find out we are not the family of five that they think we are. My biggest fear in life is being a disappointment to my children. I have tried every day since I was 19 to be the best mother I could be. No one can tell you how heavy a responsibility that is until you become a mother yourself. It is only then you get it. The weight of that role.

We went on after that court battle and grew our beautiful family together as I have written about. We built it on the foundations of those early years. Mia, as I said at the start of the book, never questioned who Daniel was. He had been around since she was a newborn baby so to her and us, he is her dad in every sense of the word. She was only a baby when that person who she was blood related to (it's the only way I see him) left her life, so she didn't remember any of it. Something I was so grateful for. She had enough to deal with growing up autistic and struggling daily. I had put it all to the back of my mind and naively being so young I thought I would never have to tell Mia anything about that time in her life. I was ignorant to the fact that your kids do grow up to be adults themselves. You're so in the thick of it when they are little that you think you can protect them forever. You fix every small issue from a scraped knee to a fight with their pals. As they turn into young people you quickly learn you can't protect them like you used to. It is one of the hardest roles of being a parent when they grow up and must figure things out for themselves. Everyone deserves to know the truth about who they are and where they came from. It wasn't my place to keep that from her. Every single day as she grew up it was on my mind, this secret we had kept from her. Every time we took a trip back home to Dublin, I would scan everywhere in case we ran into him or his family. Every time I had to get her a new passport and sign an affidavit that I was her only legal guardian I thought about it. It was in my head all the time. Behind all the other stuff we were dealing with. When Mia started going out by herself with friends up there, I would imagine someone coming up to her and saying, 'I know who you are', or 'I know your real dad', and her not having a clue what they were talking about. I could not let her hear that from anyone else. It would destroy her, and us. I think when she was younger it was easier to keep it a secret as she was with us all the time. As she got older and joined social media it would haunt me that someone would message her, or she would add someone on Instagram without knowing who they really were. I was always going to tell her, but I had to wait for the right time. I had kept written diaries of every access visit and every maintenance payment, and I hid them in a safe in my old house behind the attic wall for years so none of the children would find them until they were older. Every few months I would tell my mam and sister where they were so if anything happened to me, they would be found. My biggest fear was something would happen to me before I could tell my kids the truth. As Mia approached 18 it all suddenly came piling down on top of me that she had to be told. As did Ava and Jack. I think losing my dad at 18 gave me extra anxiety that something was going to happen to me, and they would be left with me never explaining anything. I could not damage them like that. It would be unforgivable.

It was like my soul knew it was time. I had done so much healing and work on my mental health, and now I could be at my strongest to tackle it with the kids. I also had a health scare and had to undergo a lot of tests on my heart due to family history, and that was the final straw for me. It felt like the universe was pulling everything at me to tell them the truth. Mia, Ava and Jack had grown up never knowing that Daniel was not Mia's biological father. We didn't plan it that way. So much happened when Mia was so young that I guess I naively thought we wouldn't have to face it. I didn't want my family destroyed. We were so focused on building our family unit it wasn't even on our minds when she was small. But then your kids grow up into young adults and there is no escaping the truth. Suddenly they are people with their own thoughts, opinions and feelings on life. We had worked so hard to give these three babies so much love and security. I was convinced once I told them they would hate me. I never saw it as a lie. I still don't. I see it as a mother protecting her children till the time is right to tell the story of our family. I felt the heaviness of that secret day in and day out. I lost years of sleep over it. I had so many panic attacks I lost count. It destroyed me in a lot of ways and controlled my life for a long time. I didn't see the consequences of that until it came out. I had to claw myself back up and fight the darkness a lot of days. It made me realise just how unbreakable I am when it comes to protecting my kids.

For a whole year before it came out, we discussed telling the kids. We kept trying to get to certain milestones before we ripped their world open. First it was Mia's 18th birthday, then we couldn't say anything as she was doing her leaving cert, and it was a hard year as it was to keep her physically in school, as she hated it so much. She was constantly being caught skipping school. Then she was coming out of a hard place herself with her own mental health. I didn't want to impact it anymore with our secret. We decided we would tell her when she finished school but then I got told about my health and that took over so we decided it had to be the August when I would get my results and before she headed to Dublin to college. Time was up. That entire 12 weeks up to it I was having so many tests done including CT scans, heart checks, bloods every four weeks, angiograms, liver scans, blood pressure monitors, I was seeing a genetic cardiologist and liver specialist. I was told if I didn't change my lifestyle, I wouldn't see 40. I was three stone overweight and comfort eating and drinking. My cholesterol was 7.8. My physical health was shocking. I was 38 at the time. I was convinced I was going to end up like my dad. So, I started to change my lifestyle drastically. All the while thinking of telling Mia everything. I never slept a wink. I was under so much pressure and stress. I would go over and over in my head what I would say. How I would say it. I would envision their crushed faces and the look of hatred towards us for keeping something so big from them. Daniel and I ended up in tears anytime we even tried to speak about it. We hated even saying it out loud. It broke our hearts. I felt like I was living on a ticking time bomb but trying to carry on as normal as possible so the kids wouldn't realise anything was amiss. No wonder my blood pressure was through the roof.

I would confide in my friends about it and they were my rock through it all. They would cry with me because they knew how much our children meant to us. I never wanted to break Daniel's heart either by telling them. He is the most amazing dad. A natural. The most loving, kind and patient father. He adores all his children and has never once treated Mia any differently. There are not enough words in the world to describe how truly wonderful he is. He is rare and we are so blessed to have him. I truly believe my dad sent him to me all those years ago. He is the very definition of what a dad should be, and I knew it was going to rip him apart telling Mia, but it wasn't our secret to keep. Mia had to know where she came from. Everyone deserves that. It was our responsibility as her parents to tell her that. Yet that didn't make any of it any easier. There was never going to be a right time, a right moment.

I got my health results back and thankfully there was nothing sinister now that I had taken the steps to get myself healthy. A small blockage in my neck, but nothing to worry about as long as I maintained the weight loss and the healthier lifestyle, and a check up in a year with my cardiologist. It was a huge relief. I felt like I was being given a second chance really, health-wise. We had Mia's debs then, in the middle of August, and that was the final thing to get out of the way before we told her. Every single event or celebration over the last 18 years, it was always there. Hanging over us. I cannot explain the weight of that feeling. We had kept it secret for so long that it was so surreal to finally speak about it out loud. The days kept passing by and the anxiety rose in me. My body was screaming at me to tell her. So, we picked a day and that was it. No more hiding.

It was a Friday so we would have the entire weekend with no plans to really be there for the kids. We didn't sleep a wink the night before. We spent most of it crying on and off. Daniel was absolutely terrified to tell her. He just couldn't take it on, it was destroying him. To save him some of the heartbreak I made the decision that I would speak to Mia first. I felt it was the best way. He was so relieved yet so broken. I had to do it. We started this journey just her and I and I felt it was fitting for it to be me and her at this moment. Some people didn't approve of that and I'm sure when people read it here, they also won't approve. That is not my concern. We do what works for our family. Unless you are ever in our shoes you can't possibly understand our way with our children.

I'm not going to go into too many details about that conversation. It was a very vulnerable and heart crushing moment for both of us, one that I think should be kept private. What I will say is it was the hardest thing I ever had to do. I didn't have a speech planned. I thought naively I had eighteen years to figure out a way to explain and yet I could not get my words out. I couldn't physically say it. I kept looking at her face thinking I was about to destroy everything we had built. I started at the very beginning when my dad died and went from there and I told it all. It came rolling out. Each part of it I could see play out in my mind. My heart was thumping, and my body was shaking. I kept going with it, to when I found out I was pregnant to how Daniel became her dad and to how we had built the family we had. In between the crying and the shaking I spilled out everything to her. It felt bizarre speaking to her about it. I had worked it up so much in my head over the years that it felt like I was floating out of my body and watching both of us from the sidelines. It was surreal. I cannot explain how amazing Mia was with that conversation. She very rarely shows emotion or affection but when I was finished speaking, she got up and held me so tight. We both cried heavily. I hugged her back just as tight and told her I totally understood if she hated me. She told me she could never hate me, and she understood why we had protected her the way we had.

She told me nothing had changed regarding Dan. He was her dad. I felt a weight lift off me at that moment. It was like I had been carrying around this huge ball on a chain connected to me for a lifetime and suddenly someone unlocked it, and I was free.. She could have easily lashed out at me, stormed out and went wild, but she didn't. She just kept saying she understood. I didn't think I could love her anymore than I did till we had that conversation. It sealed our bond. It didn't destroy us. She is such an amazing young woman. It could not have gone any better, but I knew this would take a long time to process. When Daniel came in, she hugged him and said he was her dad, and nothing changed, and she loved him even more. The relief and emotion on his face. We spent the next few hours the three of us talking it all through. It was so surreal sitting chatting openly about it. There were a lot of questions and we answered them all honestly, but my head was thumping from it all. It was intense. We then had to sit Ava and Jack down and tell them. I felt the anxiety and fear build up all over again.

I was worried about how Ava would take it. She is so like me, family means everything to her. She is naturally maternal and loving and I knew this would knock her for six. I did the exact same thing as I did with Mia and told them everything from the start. It felt harder the second time around because all of us were there together and I couldn't hold in my tears looking at their faces. Ava broke down and she was so shocked.

None of them had any clue Mia wasn't biologically Daniels. That's a huge testament to him. He always treated the three the exact same. Jack ran to me and hugged me so tightly that he nearly knocked me over. It meant so much to me for them to be so loving towards us after what we had just disclosed. The tears from us all seemed to fill the room. It was a huge moment for the five of us.

We spent the entire weekend in between crying and talking. There was no question we wouldn't answer honestly. That is hugely humbling as a parent. To sit there and have your children question your choices and your ways. There was so much processing and talking to do. It drained us. The three of them couldn't have taken it any better but it didn't make it any less hard. My biggest fear was that it would rip our family apart. It did the opposite. It completely bonded us together. Our family unit was unbreakable. We did it the right way for us, and most importantly we did it the right way for our children. We kept focused on making sure the three of them processed it properly over the next few months. We went on a family holiday a couple of weeks after we told them everything, and it was my first holiday in 18 years where I was not looking over my shoulder waiting on the past to jump out at us.

I felt a calmness like never before. I watched my three children and my husband together and realised nothing had changed between us. We were still the family unit we had built, just this time with no secret. It was one of my favourite trips. Over the next 11 months both Mia and Ava attended counselling. I wanted them to have every avenue of support open to them, not just us. I believe their mental health must be our priority. Jack didn't want to attend counseling. He seemed happy enough with us answering his questions but if he does, I will absolutely take him. I wanted my three children to come out of this process as unscathed as possible. That meant really being open and honest to their feelings and their opinions. No matter mine or Daniels. It was about them. We still speak about the whole thing nearly a year later. It's become part of normal conversation. It made us all so much closer, and I didn't think that was possible as we were a close family as it was. Having our children so young, myself and Dan really did grow up with them. We are unique and I love that about us.

Against all odds we created this amazing family unit, and far from destroying it we made it stronger. Mia wanted Dan to adopt her, but now that she is 19 it wasn't an option, so she legally changed her last name to his. Bittersweet. Their bond still makes me emotional anytime I see them together. It is the only thing I could have dreamed of when I was pregnant with her. Building our family has been the greatest achievement of my life. If you had told me at 19 how we would go on and conquer so much I would not have believed you. Becoming a mother saved my life. I truly believe that. It gave me a reason to be here. It also showed me that the strength of a mothers love really is unmatched.

CHAPTER 16

The After Effect

When something happens in your life, big or small, I now know there is an after effect. That shouldn't have taken me that long to realise, but it did. I seemed to live in freeze mode for a lot of these last twenty one years. Grief and trauma can do that to you. The years creep up on you, and you don't see it. I didn't see it because I went from a normal 18-year-old girl to suddenly losing her dad and becoming a mum a year later at 19. My life really did just change overnight. I had three children by the time I was twenty-five. I was so busy just getting through life I didn't realise a lot of me got stuck frozen in time. When I went to counselling, I learnt so much. I healed a lot of traumas surrounding my dad dying so young. I also healed a lot of my own trauma dealing with anxiety so much. I thought there wasn't really anything left to heal. I thought we would tell the kids our story and we would be relieved that it was out, and we could all just move on. It didn't really work out that way for me. It made us so much stronger as a family yes and thank God we all still have an amazing relationship but for me personally it has really taken a toll on me. Its opened-up wounds I didn't even realise I had.

It's been nearly a year since we told the kids and still, I am so mentally and physically exhausted. It's like my mind and body are in constant recovery from the weight of carrying such a heavy secret for all those years. Coming out the other side of not being in survival mode anymore has also unravelled in me just how hard life has been. I have really gone through every emotion possible. I have lost so much sleep and had so much anxiety that some nights I felt so low in the darkness that the bright mornings could not come quick enough. I had 19 years of trauma pouring out of me and I was not in control of it. I have an awful habit of putting on a smile and carrying on, but going through all this has ended that narrative. I can no longer hide behind that. It was time to truly heal and you cannot do that if you don't allow yourself to feel every emotion. It has been so tough. I hate that there is such a stigma around admitting motherhood is hard in general. Whether you have neurotypical children or neurodivergent ones. Why are we not allowed to say out loud that it's tough? It's the hardest job in the world. Saying it doesn't make us any less of a good mother. Saying it shows our daughters that it is ok to not always just 'get on with it'. Getting on with it creates trauma down the line that will do so much damage. I am proof of that. Telling ourselves that our fears are silly, and our feelings are not important. It's what leads to mental health issues. My mental health has been one of my hardest journeys in life and I hid it from everyone bar my husband. I didn't want people to see me struggle, to think I couldn't cope, certainly not my children or my family. Trying to heal yourself, and parent at the same time, is the most challenging thing you will ever do.

Learning that I too am autistic has really made me realise why I struggled, and continue to struggle, with a lot of things. I wish I had known when I was little that I was autistic. Maybe the world wouldn't have felt so puzzling to me. It's now taught me how to really love myself and treat myself with compassion. Doing all the self-work and healing has also taught my three children a lot. I am breaking cycles for them, so they don't have to heal from me. My goal as a mother has been to always have an open and loving home for my children. A place they are fully accepted and applauded to be who they are, and be loved unconditionally. I feel I have done that. They are my greatest accomplishment in life.

Now that they are nearly 20, 16 and 13, it's like I am coming out the other side from those chaotic early years and realising, wow, that was all tough. It has taken a toll on me, and that is okay to say. It doesn't make me a bad mother to admit it has been a trial at times over the years. I found a lot of my journey through motherhood a real struggle. Even though I know we have done our best raising them, that doesn't take away from the hardness of parenting in this generation. I never wanted my children to ever think they were a burden to me because they never were. They never made it hard. It was everything else surrounding it. There is so much negativity and toxicity around Autism and ADHD that I always tried to shield them from that. I never want them thinking they don't have a place in this world. The family we built was built around acceptance in all aspects of their lives. Unfortunately, ignorance is everywhere, especially online or just in day-to-day life. One of my biggest issues to deal with as a mother is the ignorance towards children like mine. The complete lack of empathy or wanting to learn about them. I don't think I can ever get over that. It's broken my heart on many occasions to watch others not really engage with my children, or to have no desire too. I cannot forgive that. They are the most amazing children and yet some can't see past their own ignorance. I hate that people allow that treatment when they see it. Enabling that behaviour is another thing I cannot look past. It has taken a huge toll on my mental health, being a special needs mother, and I have had to learn ways to deal with that. The mother bear in me won't allow that behaviour near my children too often. My good-hearted side wants to try to show everyone how unique and wonderful these kids are if you just took time to truly listen to them and learn from them, yet there will always be people who just don't want to. It's taken me a long time to make my peace with that side of things.

I learnt very early that all kids want is your time. Dad's death taught me all about time and how precious it is. I wish I didn't have to learn that lesson so harshly and yet it shaped me into the parent that I am. I know my children will carry that on with their own kids one day. It's a gift that is priceless. This last year has taught me that I put an awful lot of pressure on myself as a mother, and as a person in general. I think it comes from becoming a mother so young. It's an after-effect of that time of feeling so ashamed. I know I have nothing to prove and yet I was constantly trying to do better. For the first time in my life at 39 I am prioritising myself. I dedicated so many of my years to my children. It was the biggest honour of my life doing it. I have zero regrets. Now that they are older, suddenly I seem to have more time just for me. I have struggled with that. I'm feeling embarrassed even writing that. I should be delighted and yet I have felt lost. They were all I really lived for these last 19 years and now I have had to discover who I am again. No one told me how tough that would be. To find my identity other than 'mom'. It is the only version of myself that I know.

The thing about motherhood is that it changes all the time. They need you all the time for so long that you think you will never get to sit in peace again. You think you will never sleep in again. You think you'll never feel like yourself again. That saying, the days are long but the years are short, is so accurate. Those early years are so tough. Then they are constantly in extra-curricular activities so you live in your car and your weekends are full of swimming lessons, play dates and family events. You and your partner are like passing ships. Family life takes over everything. You go through different phases of losing each other at times it feels. It's all hard. That is something extra you have to work on and adds even more work to the chaos that is life. Then they hit the teen years, and you feel like you have been dragged into another world filled with hormones and stress, and it's bewildering. It is not for the faint hearted. Nothing will humble you or teach you more as a parent than having teenagers. I have three, I am living proof. I learnt more about being the right kind of parent at this stage than any other. They are figuring out who they are and you're suddenly chasing them for some time. It's all hard, no matter what stage, and once you admit that it suddenly seems lighter. You're all struggling together but at different things. When you start out in the teen years your heart will be thrown with a grieving process for that younger version of your children that could not leave you alone for two seconds. Remember all those years you could never pee alone and you dreamt of sitting in a room quietly? Now you're suddenly walking on eggshells, standing outside their door hoping you get a smile or a hello when you enter the room. You'll miss your kids and they are only in the next room. They need their own space and their own time, and you're not their number one anymore and it will break your heart but that is how it needs to be. They are growing and learning and figuring out life. It's a whole new dynamic and you're holding on for dear life. Yet you all find your way. Like everything, life goes on. You settle into this new stage and hope you're doing the right thing at the end of the day. Have I mentioned that wine helps? Just keep showing up. In whatever way they need. That is what I have learned as a mother. They don't want your advice, your judgement. They just want you there to listen and to vent to. If they ask, offer the solutions but nine times out of ten they just want comfort and support on their terms. So often over the endless teen dramas, bullying, life events I have had to count to ten in my own head, take a deep breath and remember to sit and listen first. Speak later. There are countless times I have failed at that too. That's where the humbling part comes in. They come out the otherside of all that chaos of teen years and I adore now my relationship with all three. It's the most special and important relationship in my life, bar the one with my husband.

They are my biggest cheerleaders in life, as well as my husband. It was them who pushed this book and it is them pushing me to discover who I am now. I could not have more support around me. I have everything I have ever wanted in them.

Mia, Ava and Jack, Thank you for showing me that the bravest thing you can do in life is be yourself.

Printed in Great Britain
by Amazon